# CAMBRIDGE LIBRARY COLLECTION

*Books of enduring scholarly value*

## Literary studies

This series provides a high-quality selection of early printings of literary works, textual editions, anthologies and literary criticism which are of lasting scholarly interest. Ranging from Old English to Shakespeare to early twentieth-century work from around the world, these books offer a valuable resource for scholars in reception history, textual editing, and literary studies.

## Worke for Cutlers

This edition of Worke for Cutlers was edited by Albert Forbes Sieveking and published in 1904, shortly after it had been staged (probably for the first time in 300 years) at Trinity Hall. The play was originally published anonymously in 1615, and was then described as 'Acted in a Shew in the famous Universitie of Cambridge'. Sieveking gives reasons to believe that Thomas Heywood, whose most famous work is A Woman Killed with Kindness (1603), had at least a part in its writing, and points out the topicality of a 'Merry Dialogue betweene Sword, Rapier and Dagger' at a time when James I was issuing edicts against duelling, which was punishable by heavy fines or even death. The short play is provided with a 'glossarial epilogue' containing explanatory notes.

Cambridge University Press has long been a pioneer in the reissuing of out-of-print titles from its own backlist, producing digital reprints of books that are still sought after by scholars and students but could not be reprinted economically using traditional technology. The Cambridge Library Collection extends this activity to a wider range of books which are still of importance to researchers and professionals, either for the source material they contain, or as landmarks in the history of their academic discipline.

Drawing from the world-renowned collections in the Cambridge University Library, and guided by the advice of experts in each subject area, Cambridge University Press is using state-of-the-art scanning machines in its own Printing House to capture the content of each book selected for inclusion. The files are processed to give a consistently clear, crisp image, and the books finished to the high quality standard for which the Press is recognised around the world. The latest print-on-demand technology ensures that the books will remain available indefinitely, and that orders for single or multiple copies can quickly be supplied.

The Cambridge Library Collection will bring back to life books of enduring scholarly value across a wide range of disciplines in the humanities and social sciences and in science and technology.

# Worke for Cutlers

*A Merry Dialogue betweene Sword, Rapier
and Dagger*

ALBERT FORBES SIEVEKING

CAMBRIDGE
UNIVERSITY PRESS

CAMBRIDGE UNIVERSITY PRESS

Cambridge  New York  Melbourne  Madrid  Cape Town  Singapore  São Paolo  Delhi

Published in the United States of America by Cambridge University Press, New York

www.cambridge.org
Information on this title: www.cambridge.org/9781108003117

© in this compilation Cambridge University Press 2009

This edition first published 1904
This digitally printed version 2009

ISBN 978-1-108-00311-7

# WORKE FOR CVTLERS

**Cambridge:**
PRINTED BY J. AND C. F. CLAY,
AT THE UNIVERSITY PRESS.

## By the King.

**¶ A Proclamation againſt priuate Challenges and**
Combats : VVith Articles annexed for the better directions to
be vſed thereIn, and for the more iudiciall proceeding againſt Offenders.

He ſlaughters which We find to haue bene ſtrangely multiplied and encreaſed in theſe later times, by the boldneſſe which many of Our ſubiects take, to chalenge any man into the Field, towards whom they cary either grudge or malice in their minds, vnder the pretext of ſatiſfaction to pretended wrongs, without imploring aide either of the Lawes, or Ciuil Magiſtrates: haue mooued Us, out of the tender care which we take of Our loyall Subiects liues, to enter into ſome ſpeedie courſe for the ſtopping of a Uaine that bleeds both inceſſantly, and inwardly. For to ſpeake trueth, to what purpoſe ſerue the Lawes of God, the prouiſionall inſtructions of men, and the courſe of ordinarie Juſtice in the Common wealth (whether wee reſpect the Court of Chiualrie, or the Ciuill Courts,) if it be free for Subiects out of the diſtemper of their owne diſtempered conceits, either to rate the quality of the wrong ſuppoſed, or the ſatiſfaction that belongs to it: Beſides, it were great pittie, that ſo many Judgements as in other things ſhew grauitie and moderation, ſhould be ſo ſtrangely bewitched, and as it were enchanted in this kinde with the very dregges of Circes Cup. (transforming conſideration into paſſion, reaſon into appetite, and men into beaſts) as to thinke that any graine of worth of reputation or true honour, can be drawne out of any act that is abſolutely repugnant to all ſuch Lawes (aſwell Diuine as humane) as ſway both Religions and Poliſies. For as no man accompts his Armour of high proofe, before it haue bene tried by Shot no more are Gentlemen eſteemed for their valour by the greater part of giddie cenſours at this day, that haue not almoſt aſſoone as they can hold a Sword in their hand, put themſelues vpon their proofe, either in S.Georges fields, or at Finsbury, without the leaſt reſpect to the Juſtice of the ground that ſhould make good the purſuit or euent of the quarrell.

WE are not ignorant in what degree ſlaughters vpon priuate Challenges are ranked by the Lawes of the land, (howſoeuer ſinſurie be made the maſke) nor how earneſt many buſie perſons are to make their owne wills abſolute in ſome point, ſince they know not by what colour or pretence to command in all, nor how cunningly ſome argue for excuſe of Challenges, by imputing weakeneſſe (as they would haue vs apprehend) to the Lawes and Statutes of the Realme, in that they forbeare either out of inſenſibilitie or neglect, to giue ſatiſfaction to ſome certaine termes and reproches, As for example to that of the Lye, which the cuſtome and conſtruction of the dayes in which wee liue hath matched with thoſe wrongs that are reputed to be moſt exorbitant : For though no priuate Challenge to the peril of a loyall Subiects life, be either iuſt or compatible with

*Reduced Facsimile of first page of King James I.'s Proclamation* A.D. 1613. (*From a photograph by Mr George Clinch, with permission of the Society of Antiquaries.*)

# WORKE FOR CVTLERS

## Or A Merry Dialogue betweene
## Sword, Rapier and Dagger.

*Acted in a Shew in the famous Universitie of Cambridge* A.D. 1615.

Edited, with Historical Prologue and Glossarial Epilogue,

BY

### ALBERT FORBES SIEVEKING,

F.S.A., F.R.Hist.S., S.S.C., and Author of "The Praise of Gardens."

With Introductory Note by

### Dr A. W. WARD,

Facsimiles of Proclamation of 1613, and Two Play Bills.

It is a common practice nowadayes amongst a sort of shifting companions, that runne through euery art, and thriue by none, to leaue the trade of *Nouerint* whereto they were borne, and busie themselues with the indeuors of art.

NASH's Address prefixed to GREENE's *Arcadia or Menaphon.*

LONDON :

C. J. CLAY AND SONS,
Cambridge University Press Warehouse,
Ave Maria Lane

1904

London: C. J. CLAY AND SONS,
CAMBRIDGE UNIVERSITY PRESS WAREHOUSE,
AVE MARIA LANE.
Glasgow: 50, WELLINGTON STREET.

Leipzig: F. A. BROCKHAUS.
New York: THE MACMILLAN COMPANY.
Bombay and Calcutta: MACMILLAN AND CO., Ltd.

TO THE GENTLEMEN STUDENTS OF THE FAMOUS
UNIVERSITIE OF CAMBRIDGE,

and to the Fellows of Trinity Hall and the Royal Historical Society,
who, as shewn in the two Play Bills, most hospitably welcomed
"Worke for Cutlers" back to dramatic life.

A sweet touch, a quick venew of wit,—snip snap, quick and home!

*Love's Labour's Lost.*

Fungar vice cotis, acutum
Reddere quae ferrum valet exsors ipsa secandi.

Horace.

Yet in writing this book, some men will marvel perchance, why that I, being an unperfect Shooter, should take in hand to write of making a perfect Archer: the same man, peradventure, will marvel how a whetstone, which is blunt, can make the edge of a knife sharp.

Then in fence also, men are taught to go about that thing, which the best of them all knoweth he shall never attain unto.

Roger Ascham's *Toxophilus*, 1545.

# AT TRINITY HALL, CAMBRIDGE
*(by the courtesy of the Master and Fellows)*

This present Thursday, July 23rd, 1903, at 4 o'clock

Will be Presented Tudor Sword-Play by Captain ALFRED HUTTON, F.S.A., and Mr T. H. TOYNBEE.

and will be Re-Presented WORKE FOR CVTLERS, a Jacobean Dialogue (last "Acted in a Shew in the Famous Universitie of Cambridge" A.D. 1615) revived by A. FORBES SIEVEKING, F.S.A.

and will be Performed A Consort of Music by English Composers of the Elizabethan period upon the Lute, the Virginals, and the Treble and Bass Viols, under the direction of Mr ARNOLD DOLMETSCH.

1. Pavan and Galliard for the Treble Viol, Bass Viol and Virginals:
   *"The Lord of Salisbury."*    *William Byrd.*
   *Treble Viol: Mr Arnold Dolmetsch.*
   *Bass Viol: Miss Mabel Johnston.*
   *Virginals: Miss Kelly.*

2. Broad Sword and Buckler.

3. Two Pieces for the Bass Viol accompanied by the Virginals:
   i. *"A Tune."*
   ii. *"Heart's Ease." Anonymous.*
   *Miss Mabel Johnston and Mr Arnold Dolmetsch.*

4. Dagger *v.* Unarmed Man.

5. Two Pieces for the Lute:
   i. *"The Buffens."*
   ii. *"Canaries." Anonymous.*
   *Mr Arnold Dolmetsch.*

   Two Songs accompanied by the Lute:
   i. *"O Willo Willo."*
   ii. *"Have you seen but a whyte Lillie grow." Anonymous. Words by Ben Jonson.*
   *Miss Van Wagner and Mr Arnold Dolmetsch.*

6. WORKE FOR CVTLERS: or a Merry Dialogue betweene
   Sword .........*Mr A. G. Ross.*
   Rapier .........*Mr M. Compton Mackenzie.*
   Dagger.........*Mr A. Forbes Sieveking.*

7. Two pieces for the Treble Viol accompanied by the Virginals:
   i. *"Fortune."*
   ii. *"Green Sleeves." Anonymous.*
   *Mr Arnold Dolmetsch and Miss Mabel Johnston.*

8. Case of Rapiers.
   Pages: Masters R. and F. B. SEDGWICK.

9. Two Fantazies for Two Viols:
   i. *Fantazie.*
      *"Alfonso Coperario."*
   ii. *"La Caccia."*
      *Thomas Morley.*

10. Rapier and Dagger.

11. A Song accompanied by Two Viols and the Virginals:
    *"O Mistress Mine." Anonymous. Words by Shakespeare.*
    *Miss Van Wagner, Mr Arnold Dolmetsch, Miss Mabel Johnston and Miss Kelly.*

**DEUS SERVET REGEM ET REGNUM**

# INTRODUCTORY NOTE.

Mr Forbes Sieveking's valuable contribution to a field of literary research which notwithstanding its many attractions still remains relatively neglected needs, I am sure, no commendation on my part. To begin with, this scholarly edition, alike instructive and suggestive, of a very curious and very creditable specimen —shall I say of University wit or of wit suitable for University consumption?—will be welcomed by many Cambridge readers as a pleasant reminiscence. Last summer, the performance of *Worke for Cutlers*, when Sword, Rapier and Dagger carried on their subtle contention in the open, set the crown upon the pleasant hospitalities of a Long Vacation afternoon spent in the congenial surroundings of Trinity Hall. And, remembering how near we were to Clare and Trinity and St John's, some of us could not on the occasion repress the wish that in these days, when there is so much theatre of one kind or another, 'shews' bringing to mind the polite recreations of our predecessors were more frequent; and that the revival *in loco* of this 'merry dialogue' might lead to the reproduction of some full-blown specimens of a far from insignificant literary growth—our native academical drama. *Worke for Cutlers* dates from a period in our University history signally memorable in respect of its efforts in this direction; for it was printed in the very year of the famous royal visit to Cambridge, during which among other plays *Ignoramus* and *Albumazar* were performed; and, when one comes to think of it, Oliver Cromwell, who is fabled to have filled a part in a much earlier academical comedy, only came up a year or so too late to have a chance of playing Sword.   But the savour of this dialogue is of Court and Town as well as of the University; or perhaps it might be said that its matter is of the former, though its manner makes special appeal to the kind of trained intelligence necessarily abounding in the Universities and in the Inns of Court. Mr Forbes Sieveking has ventured on a highly ingenious conjecture which suits both ingredients in the product; but though I have every reason for welcoming any addition to the literary reputation of Thomas Heywood, I must for the present be content with advising that this Dialogue be placed in the Library of my College as a 'doubtful' work of one of its worthies.   Thomas Heywood would have been capable of this *tour de force*, no doubt; for his range was wide, and his versatility was part, though not the most characteristic part, of himself.

The historical value of this little piece is by no means trifling; for, as Mr Forbes Sieveking has made clear, King James I.'s Edict against Duels gives its point to the discussion, and this Edict marks an important stage in the gradual evolution of a social reform for which there is reason enough to bless the Pacific King's name.   The literary characteristics of the dialogue are on the surface, but they deserve attention for their own sake.   Just as so large an amount of professorial insight into the entire philosophy and art of the practice of single combat was sure sooner or later to lead to its ultimate suppression as a national institution or custom —so an excess of verbal wit which overlaid everything with its too well-meant efforts could not but stifle what dramatic possibilities there lay in such a dialogue.   In truth it is best enjoyed in print; and to do itself full justice, it needs the expenditure of technical and antiquarian lore which it has been fortunate enough to receive at the hands of its present editor.

A. W. WARD.

PETERHOUSE LODGE,
  *March,* 1904.

# Royal Historical Society.

*At the Hall of the Honourable Society of Gray's Inn.*
*By permission of the Treasurer, Edward Dicey, Esq., C.B., and*
*Masters of the Bench*

On Thursday, January 7th, 1904, at 5 o'clock in the afternoon,

A Concert of Seventeenth Century English Music will be performed
by Mr. W. A. BOXALL and Mr. W. SUTCLIFFE (Violins), Mr. J.
ANSELL (Viola), Mr. B. PATTERSON PARKER (Violoncello), and
Miss ENID GABELL (Singer);

Tudor Sword-Play will be presented by Captain CYRIL G. R.
MATTHEY, F.S.A., and Mr. T. H. TOYNBEE;

And a Jacobean Dialogue, entitled WORKE FOR CUTLERS,
first acted at the University of Cambridge A.D. 1615, will be
revived under the direction of Mr. A. FORBES SIEVEKING, F.S.A.,
F.R.Hist.S.

I. Music from the Masque
"Cupid and Death," by
Matthew Locke (1628–
1677).

II. 𝔅𝔯𝔬𝔞𝔡 𝔖𝔴𝔬𝔯𝔡 𝔞𝔫𝔡 𝔅𝔲𝔠𝔨𝔩𝔢𝔯,
against 𝔅𝔯𝔬𝔞𝔡 𝔖𝔴𝔬𝔯𝔡
𝔞𝔫𝔡 𝔇𝔞𝔤𝔤𝔢𝔯, 𝔞𝔰 𝔱𝔞𝔲𝔤𝔥𝔱
𝔟𝔶 𝔊𝔢𝔬𝔯𝔤𝔢 𝔖𝔦𝔩𝔟𝔢𝔯 𝔦𝔫
𝔥𝔦𝔰 "𝔓𝔞𝔯𝔞𝔡𝔬𝔯𝔢𝔰 𝔬𝔣 𝔇𝔢-
𝔣𝔢𝔫𝔠𝔢," 1599.

*From Jacob Sutor's "Künstliches Fechtbuch," 1612*

III. Ayre, Corant, and Saraband, by John Jenkins (1592–1678).

IV. Miss Enid Gabell:
  (a) *"Dear, thy face is Heav'n to me."*
  (b) *"Go, young man, let my heart alone."* } Henry Lawes, 1658.

V. 𝔄 𝔠𝔞𝔰𝔱 𝔬𝔣 𝔯𝔞𝔭𝔦𝔢𝔯𝔰 (right and left hands) 𝔞𝔠𝔠𝔬𝔯𝔡𝔦𝔫𝔤 𝔱𝔬 𝔙𝔦𝔫𝔠𝔢𝔫𝔱𝔦𝔬
𝔖𝔞𝔳𝔦𝔬𝔩𝔬, 𝔥𝔦𝔰 𝔓𝔯𝔞𝔠𝔱𝔦𝔰𝔢, 1595.

VI. Music from "Cupid and
Death," by Matthew
Locke.

VII. Preludio, and Song-Tune
composed for the
Lute by Henry Pur-
cell, 1658–1695, and
"Canaries" (Anon.).

VIII. 𝔯𝔞𝔭𝔦𝔢𝔯 𝔞𝔫𝔡 𝔇𝔞𝔤𝔤𝔢𝔯.

IX. WORKE FOR CUTLERS, or a Merry Dialogue
  (Ascribed to Thomas Heywood).

  Sword ..................*Mr. A. G. Ross.*
  Rapier ..................*Mr. Edward G. Eliot.*
  Dagger..................*Mr. A. Forbes Sieveking.*
  Pages  Masters F. B. Sedgwick and Cecil Spriggs

X. Aire and Contre Danse, by Henry Purcell
  Music from "Cupid and Death," by Matthew Locke.

XI. Miss Enid Gabell .
  (a) *When I am laid in earth.*
    *From "Dido and Aeneas."* } Henry Purcell,
  (b) *Kind Fortune smiles.* 1675.

XII. God Save the King, by Dr. John Bull (1563–1628).

# PROLOGUE.

The following reprint of what, taking a hint from Beaumont and Fletcher, may be called a Combat of "Wit at several Weapons," or, in still earlier language, a "Wappenschaw"—is from one of the rarest of early English plays, if so minute an opuscule may assert a claim to so dignified a title. My attention being drawn to *Worke for Cutlers* in the modernised version of the *Harleian Miscellany* (10 vols. 4°, 1808—13)[1], I at first naturally accepted the current belief that the only known copy of the original (of which this is an exact line-for-line and word-for-word reproduction) was the one in the British Museum.

But the bibliographical curiosity of my friend, Mr M. Compton Mackenzie of Magdalen College, Oxford, discovered another example in the Library of Worcester College, and the courtesy of its Librarian, Mr H. A. Pottinger, has enabled me to identify a twin copy, alike in all respects.—The first reprint with modernised spelling was given in vol. x. of the *Harleian Miscellany* under the editorship of Thomas Park, with the following brief introduction :—

That punning species of gladiatorial wit, with which the following dramatic dialogues abound, is likely to have procured them academical admirers, in the time of our first James, when scarce a word—

> "to royal favour had pretence
> But what agreed in sound, and clashed in sense."

The particular occasion which introduced these pieces as parts of a University shew does not appear : but they are curious specimens of the taste of a former age in its scholastic entertainments.

---

[1] It is not in Oldys's original edition in 8 vols., 4°, 1744—6.

It was next, I believe, reproduced (evidently from the copy of 1615) by Mr Charles Hindley with other tracts, under the general title of *Miscellanea Antiqua Anglicana* and the better known sub-title of *The Old Book Collector's Miscellany*, 3 vols. (Reeves and Turner). In vol. 2 is also given another *Merry Dialogue* on precisely similar lines, evidently from the same hand, or some other deliberately imitating it—the very turns of the sentences and the expressions and phrases bearing a close resemblance. Its full title is as follows:—"A Merry Dialogue between Band, Cuffe and Ruff.—Done by an excellent wit, and lately acted in a Shew in the famous Universitie of Cambridge. London, printed by W. Stansby for Miles Patrick and are to be sold at his Shop neare Saint Dunstone's Churchyard in Fleet Street, 1615" (11 pp.). This is also contained in the same vol. of the *Harleian Miscellany*[1].

But between these two issues of *Worke for Cutlers*, allusion had been made to it in an able and original article in the *Retrospective Review*, as follows:—

*The Returne from Parnassus* was called by its Author a *Show*. In 1615 another was performed, entitled *Worke for Cutlers*...its author is unknown, and the interlude itself almost equally so; it may be classed among the very scarcest of the early English dramas[2].

The title may have been inspired by Thomas Dekker's *Worke for Armorours: or The Peace is broken* (1609), from which I take the following extract bearing upon our subject:

"*Cutlers* and *Armorers* have got more by them (the *Hollander* and

---

[1] The Second Edition (also in 1615) is called "*Exchange Ware and the Second Hand*, viz. Band Ruffe and Cuffe, lately cut, and now newly dearned up, or a Dialogue, acted in a Shew in the Famous Universitie of Cambridge. The Second Edition. London. Printed by W. Stansby for Myles Patrick, and are to be sold at his Shop, neere Saint Dunstanes Church Yard, in Fleet Street. 1615.

[2] *The Retrospective Review*, 1825. Vol. xii. p. 1, Art. "The Latin Plays acted before the University of Cambridge." (For this reference, and for several other valuable ones, I am indebted to Mr J. Bass Mullinger, the latest and most philosophical historian of the University, whose chapter on the Academic Drama is, like the rest of the work, full of original research and critical insight.)

the *Spaniard*) within these few yeares, then by any fowre Nation (besides them) in Christendome all their whole liues."

A few words of speculation in regard to the unknown author may perhaps be allowed me. Having no reputation for historical scholarship to jeopardise, I venture to hazard the daring opinion that this *Merry Dialogue* may be from the pen of no less a dramatist than Thomas Heywood himself. So much for irresponsible free-lancedom in dogmatic criticism—*credo, ergo est.* Having, however, a certain respect for what amongst lawyers is called "the weight of evidence" (with whatever levity of argument it may be adduced), I feel it desirable to give my sparse reasons as concisely as possible for the faith that is in me.

1. There is evidence that Thomas Heywood was at one time a resident at Cambridge; and it is probable that he was a member of Peterhouse. Wm Cartwright says definitely that he was a Fellow of that College.

By Heywood's own confession, (in the Preface to the *English Traveller*), he had a hand in no less than 220 plays. "This tragic comedy, (being one reserved amongst 220) in which I had either the entire hand or at least a main finger, coming accidentally to the press." Moreover he was notoriously careless of his own fame, living or posthumous, although he is unwilling to let the play in question pass as "*Filius Populi*—a Bastard without a father." He continues, "True it is that my plays are not exposed to the world in Volumes, to bear the title of works (as others)"—Charles Lamb comments "he seems to glance at Ben Jonson"—one reason being that "many of them by shifting and change of companies, have been negligently lost—others of them are still retained in the hands of some actors who think it against their peculiar profit to have them come in print, and a third that it never was any great ambition in me to be in this kind voluminously read."

Upon this, Charles Lamb, who first threw open to us moderns the gates of the rich and royal domain of Elizabethan drama, makes this further remark:—

Of the 220 pieces which he here speaks of as having been concerned in, only 25, as enumerated by Dodsley, have come down to us, for the reasons assigned in the preface. The rest have perished, exposed to the casualties of a theatre. Heywood's ambition seems to have been confined to the pleasure of hearing the players speak his lines while he lived. It does not appear that he ever contemplated the possibility of being read by after ages. What a slender pittance of fame was motive sufficient to the production of such Plays as the *English Traveller*, the *Challenge for Beauty*, and the *Woman Killed with Kindness*! Posterity is bound to take care that a writer loses nothing by such a noble modesty.

Heywood, indeed, seems to have regarded it almost as a dishonest act to print his plays as well as to act them; for in the Preface to his *Rape of Lucrece* (fourth impression 1630) he makes the following explanation :

Though some have used a double sale of their labours, first to the stage, and after to the press, for my own part, I here proclaim myself ever faithful to the first, and never guilty of the last; yet since some of my plays have, unknown to me, and without any of my direction, accidentally come into the Printers hands, and therefore so corrupt and mangled, copied only by the ear, that I have been as unable to know them, as ashamed to challenge them.

And in the Prologue to a play of his, entitled *If you know not me, you know nobody*[1] (1623 edition), Heywood has the following lines :

> 'Twas ill nurst
> And yet receiv'd as well perform'd at first,
> Grac'd and frequented; for the cradle age
> Did throng the seats, the boxes, and the stage,
> So much, that some by stenography drew
> The plot, put it in print, scarce one word true:
> And in that lameness it has limp'd so long,
> The author now, to vindicate that wrong,
> Hath took the pains upright upon his feet
> To teach it walk, so please you sit and see it.

2.  In Heywood's *Apologie for Actors* dated 1612 we read in book 1:

In the time of my residence in Cambridge I have seen tragedyes, comedyes, historyes, pastorals, and *Shewes* publicly acted in which the graduates of good place and reputation have been specially parted.

[1] See p. 45 for 'Nobody' twice.

(Note that he uses the very word *Shewe* applied to this *Merry Dialogue*.)

3. Heywood was the author of a play called *Cutting Dick* now lost (see Epilogue, p. 62).

In the text (page 42) Rapier says "Did you nere heare of *Cutting-Dicke*, this is the very same man."

This, I contend, has very little point, unless Heywood was either the author of *Worke for Cutlers*, the player of the part of "Sword"— or both.

4. As Heywood was one of Her Majesty's (Queen Anne's) Players, in which capacity he attended her funeral, nothing is more probable than that he may have been in James I.'s train, when he visited Cambridge in 1615; and if he were the author of the play (which in certain respects may be regarded as a "skit" upon James I.'s Edict against Duels), there would be every reason for his not acknowledging the authorship; and the possible suppression of copies when printed after the performance would account for their rarity.

5. In others of Heywood's few extant works I find several of the puns and expressions recurring—e.g. that on "Matches" in his play *If you know not me, you know nobody*, 1605.

I think I have met with a better commodity than Matches, and my master cannot say *but he hath met with his match*.

And later on in the same play the word "match" is again punned upon.

6. *'S foot* and *God's foot* are favourite oaths with Heywood, whereas Shakspeare, I believe, only once employs this form of strong speech[1].

7. The *Dagger in Cheap* is not of frequent mention in the contemporary dramatic literature, but I do find it spoken of elsewhere by Heywood: e.g. 2nd Prentice in *If you know not me* &c. (1605). p. 76 *post*.

[1] I owe this instance (not given in Littledale's edition of Dyce's "Glossary" 1902) to Mr F. G. Fleay, who from memory referred me to *Troilus and Cressida* Act II. Sc. 3, *Thersites*, "'S foot, I'll learn to conjure and raise devils."

The "Dagger" in Holborn was a far better known hostelry and more often alluded to. In the notes I give my reasons for believing that "the Dagger in Cheap" was not in "Cheapside" itself as usually asserted by later commentators, but in Foster Lane, Cheapside (though in Farringdon Ward); and I fancy that "Cheap" is always, or nearly so, used as a district or ward, and not as an individual street.

8. I seem to trace in Heywood's earlier extant works an enthusiasm for the sword and the exercise of arms (notably in his *Foure Prentises of London*, first printed in 1632 but written 15 or 16 years before, thus bringing it very near the date of our Dialogue) which is in keeping with this supposed authorship: thus for instance:

> *Eustace.* "I am a *Grocer*: Yet had rather see
>             A faire guilt sword hung in a velvet sheath
>             Than the best Barbary Sugar in the world"

or :—

> "I would fast from meate and drinke a Summers day
>  To see Swords clash, or view a desperate fray"

or again :—

> "I am no sooner got into the Fencen-Schoole,
>  To play a venew with some friend, I bring;
>  But *Eustace*, *Eustace*, all the street must ring."

I admit that the aggregate of these crumbs of collateral argument does not form a solid crust of proof; but as the great Charles Darwin once said to me (when I told him that a certain Doctor was commonly regarded as a Dane, because he was appointed physician to the Princess of Wales on her first coming to England):—"The world accepts many things of greater importance on more slender evidence[1]."

As an instance of this, I find it stated in Fleay's *Chronicle of the English Drama* (1559—1642) that the *Siege of London* is assumed to be

---

[1] As I have no desire to figure in however distant a manner as a follower of the fanatics, who by means of cyphers set common sense and literary conscience at naught, I confess frankly that I do not detect any cryptic sign in the play confirming my contention.

Heywood's by Collier, Halliwell, the *Biographia Dramatica* and Gildon—
" I know not why," comments Mr Fleay, "unless it be that in Sc. II.
Hobs the Tanner says : 'Dost thou not know me? then thou knowest
nobody '."

With the further remark that the following entry of the publication
of the Dialogue is to be found in the Stationers' Registers—

4°. Julii. 1615.

RICHARD MEIGHEN.  Entred for his copie under the handes of Master
TAVERNOR and Master *Leake* Warden a little thing called *Worke
for Cutlers* ................................................................vjd.

and that its printer, Thomas Creede, was also the printer of the first
Quartos of *Richard III.* (1598), *Romeo and Juliet* (1599) and *Henry V.*
(1600), his name being found frequently in the Stationers' Register
between the years 1593 and 1616[1]—I now leave this part of my subject
to the credulity and criticism of my readers.

I should have liked to adduce a few more historical and enlightening
facts in regard to the ancient City Gild or Company of Cutlers ; but
it is well known that its records, owing chiefly to the Great Fire, are
not capable of yielding a very fertile crop of information as to its early
history and connection with the *Dramatis Personae* of the dialogue.
There is the well-known passage in Stow's *Survey* :—

In Horsebridge Street is the Cutler's Hall.  Richard de Wilehale 1295 confirmed
to Paul Butelar this house and edifices in the Parish of St Michael &c....paying
yearly one clove of Gereflowers (gilliflowers) at Easter.  They of this Company
were of old time divided into three arts or sorts of workmen : to wit, the first were
smiths, forgers of blades, and therefore called bladers, and divers of them proved
wealthy men....The second were makers of hafts, and otherwise garnishers of blades.
The third sort were sheathmakers, for swords, daggers and knives.  In the 10th of
Henry IV. certain ordinancies were made betwixt the bladers and the other cutlers,
and in the 4th of Henry VI. they were all three Companies drawn into one fraternity
or brotherhood by the name of Cutlers.

---

[1] I have in my library a folio translation of Macchiavelli's *Florentine History* by
Thomas Bedingfield (the translator of Claudio Corte's *Book of Horsemanship*) printed
by Thomas Creede for William Ponsonby, 1595.

I subjoin a few more early references to them from H. T. Riley's
*Memorials of London* :—

Also,—in order to avoid deceit of the people in this behalf, be it ordained that
no handle of wood, except *digeon* shall be coloured."

Ordinances of the Cutlers from the Norman-<br>French. 3 Richard II., A.D. 1380.

Every knife is prepared separately by 3 different crafts, first the blade by Smiths
called *Bladsmythes*, the handle and the other fitting work by the Cutlers, and the
sheath by the Sheathers.

> A joint petition of Cutlers and Bladesmiths showing that foreign
> folk from divers parts of England counterfeited and forged the
> marks of the Bladesmiths free of the City.

And in the same year the Articles of the Bladesmiths declared

that every person of the said trade who is a worker or maker of lance-heads,
swords, daggers or knives must make the points and egges thereof hard throughout
to stand the assay ; on pain of forfeiture thereof; also that every master shall put his
own mark upon his work.　　　　　　　　10 Henry IV., A.D. 1408.

In a letter dated 28th April, 1580, from William, Lord Burleigh, to
the Lord Mayor, we read how :

He had caused search to be made among the Cutlers in Westminster for swords
and daggers exceeding the length limited by her Majesty's Proclamation.

Finding some disorders there in having blades in their shops contrary to the said
Proclamation, the Cutlers had excused themselves, alleging that others of the same
trade in London sold both swords and daggers exceeding the length prescribed.
He requested that search should be made, and no one permitted to have any blades
in their shops not reformed according to the before mentioned Order (*Remembrancia
of the City of London*)[1].

And the following passage from Greene's *A Quip for an upstart
Courtier* (1592) shows that the average Cutler's morality was not beyond
suspicion :

And you, cutler, you are patron to ruffians and swash-bucklers, and will sell
them a blade that may be thrust into a bushel; but if a poor man, that cannot

[1] For this and another reference I am indebted to Mr Charles Welch, the Guild-
hall Librarian, and Member of the Court of the Cutlers' Company.

skill of it, you sell him a Sword or a rapier new overglazed, and swear the blade came either from Turkey or Toledo.

Let us now pass to the consideration of the state of duelling in England prior to and at the period of our Dialogue, and the weapons by which an appeal to arms in private quarrels was decided.

The duel, as is well known, sprang out of the ancient "Trial by Combat," in which the weapons appointed were " Gleyve, long-swerd, short-swerd and Dagger[1]." According to Dugdale[2], after the bill of challenge is delivered with a gauntlet to the Court by the appellant and the defendant has accepted the gauntlet and denied the point of the bill, the place is appointed, and the lists and counter lists (for the marshals) are set up. The appellant appeared at the east gate of the lists, " where he is admitted to enter by the Marshall himself, together with his Arms, Weapon, Victual, and also his Councel with him: and then is brought to a certain place within the lists, where he attends the coming of the Defendant." The marshal then measures the weapons, administers the oaths, the lists are cleared, and the constable and marshal, sitting at the King's feet, pronounce these words with a high voice: *Lesses* (Laissez) *les aller ; Lesses les aller ; Lesses les aller et faire leur devoir*[3].

In the reign of Henry VIII. (A.D. 1540) we find first mention of a corporation of the Maisters of the Science of Defence : but there is a MS. in the British Museum[4] forming a Chronicle (believed to have been compiled under Elizabeth, but commencing in the reign of Edward VI.) of a recognised and chartered body, consisting of

[1] Ex vetustate Codice MS. in Biblioth. Seldeniana.

[2] *Origines Iuridiciales*, chap. xxvi., Trial by Combat in cases Civil, and chap. xxviii. in cases Criminal; and Selden, *The Duello or Single Combate*, 1610.

[3] From a MS. book, sometime belonging to Sir Edward Wyndham, Kt, Marshal of the Camp to King Henry the Eighth.

[4] Sloane MSS., No. 2530. I was arranging for the transcription of this, in the belief that only extracts had hitherto been made, when I found on referring to *The Sword and the Centuries* (Bk IV., chap. xxv.) that my friend, Captain Alfred Hutton, had already made practically the whole accessible to his readers.

Masters, Provosts and Scholars, who formed a sort of College or Gild of Arms, bound by indentures, oaths, " ruills and constitucons." This Gild conferred degrees of proficiency upon its members after a system of practical examinations, tested by competitions at each stage of their professional careers.

The pardon craved for a " Scholar's Prize," in the tag at the conclusion of the Dialogue, undoubtedly alludes to "the Order for playinge of a Scholler's Prize," which consisted in his competing with at least six scholars at the long-sword and back-sword " for a tryall or proofe," before his admission as " a free Scholar "—and 7 years later he was qualified to play his Provost Prize, for which promotion he had to show proficiency with the two-hand sword, the back-sword and staff " with all manner of Provosts,"—the final degree for a Master's Prize being conferred upon his showing mastery of the two-hand sword, the bastard sword (sometimes now called the "hand and a half sword"), the pike, the back-sword, and the rapier and dagger. The last entry in the book is dated 1583, soon after which date a proclamation of Elizabeth dissolved the gild, in the interests of the peace and " good manners."

To take these weapons in their order of priority in the Dialogue.

The word Sword, besides its present generic meaning, implied in its earlier specific sense a heavy edged weapon used almost entirely for cutting or hacking, and generally wielded, or, in the case of the lighter bastard sword, capable of being wielded, by two hands : and it is clear from several passages in the text of the Dialogue, that even as late as the year 1615 the old conservative view of a two-handed sword being the genuine British weapon still prevailed, and that the pointed rapier was looked upon in the dubious light of a foreign *parvenu*. I am indebted to Mr Edwin Ward[1] for an analysis of the Dialogue from this point of view, and I venture to quote his letter at length, as it helps

[1] Whose acquaintance I had the pleasure of making while he was engaged in cataloguing and arranging the interesting Noel Paton collection of Arms and Armour in the Edinburgh Museum of Science and Art.

to a better understanding of the relations of the two disputants (Sword and Rapier) and their umpire (Dagger) :

The very existence of this work proves what a popular topic was the relative merits of these weapons at this period. In the Dialogue, I presume "Dagger" represents the general public opinion, and though he acknowledges the good points of both weapons, yet he evidently had strong leanings towards the classic two-handed sword as representing the king of arms with a noble pedigree, though confessing "Rapier is a Souldier, and a Man as well armed at all poynts as anie one." The only detrimental statement Dagger makes with regard to Sword is "Away Sworde, the Time was indeed when thou wast a notable Swashbuckler, but now thou art growne olde Sword." I take this to mean that about the time 1615, duels or contests, fought out with the large knightly two-handed sword, were of far less frequent occurrence than in the previous century, owing to the handy rapier having usurped the duties of the noble sword in this respect. Dagger seems to regret this from a sentimental point of view; his regard for Sword comes out later on in "Sworde, by the very sounding of his name, should bee the better Gentleman &c.," and in the same breath "Rapier hath but one arme," meaning to contrast this fact with the two hands of the sword, which he does in plain words later on. This comparison, however, viz., "You know you are two-handed Sworde, and Rapier has but one hand,...and yet youde have him go into the Fieldes with you," seems to be the beginning of the peroration or judgment of Dagger, who wishes to bring the discussion to an amicable settlement in favour of the sword, and thus magnifies the discrepancy between the two arms to please Sword, intending afterwards to easily "square" the tricky parvenu Rapier, by telling him since duels are put down (implying of course that in these he was of consequence) that he can assume the rôle of an elegant ornament and rest in peace, but that after all for serious fighting in warfare, the sword was "the weapon." One could almost imagine cheers from the ultra-conservative portion of the "house" greeting this statement. The most impartial statement made by Dagger is "Your both of one blood, only thers this difference, that Sword comes of the elder brother, and you Rapier of the younger." I consider this statement important, as Dagger admits a connection of Rapier with the true sword, two-handed even, and does not look on him as a rank outsider.

I venture to endeavour to trace this suggestion in two expressions elsewhere in the Dialogue, viz., first words of Rapier...."Nay Backe-Sword" and also "Alas I haue knowne you beare a Basket Sword." Rapier of course means to be insulting, but yet the word "sword" is coupled with Backe- and Basket as if usual expressions, and Rapier further in these expressions insinuates that even the great Sword family stepped down sometimes from their high pedestal of "two-handedness" (if this

Erinism may be permitted) to adapt themselves to the more handy form of a
Backsword or Basket sword; is this the transition from the science of simple
sweeping strokes to the intricate one of fencing?

Without laying any weight on the above statements, I think the word "sword"
was evidently used to designate the cutting weapon, either two-handed, or back or
basket variety, the first most legitimately; the rapier, though possibly indirectly
connected with the parent sword, was so far removed as to be considered a distinct
weapon (thrusting being its essential point) and therefore incorrectly or loosely
named, when called a sword. I consider you establish a fresh point in bringing into
prominence the prestige of the large two-handed weapon, which seems to be
generally thought of as something abnormal, and not as it appears to have been, the
recognised standard arm of the soldier of Elizabethan and previous times.

In the Middle Ages, the Sword was personal and personified. The
sword of Charlemagne was called *Joyeuse*, that of Roland *Durandal*, that
of Renaud *Flambaud*, that of Oliver *Hauteclaire*. Roland addresses his
sword at Roncevaux, so does Bayard after being knighted by Francis I.
and the Cid in the *Romancero*.

> "La grande épée à mains brille au croc de la selle,
>   La hache est sur le dos, la dague est sous l'aisselle."
>                             Victor Hugo, *Eviradnus*.

The first introduction of the Rapier into England is attributed, on
the authority of Camden, to Rowland Yorke in the year 1587[1].

---

[1] A.D. 1579. The long fencing rapier is described in Bullein's *Dialogue betoveen
Governesse and Chirurge* as a new kind of instrument. (See note in Wheatley's
Ben Jonson's *Every man in his Humour*.)

It is "probable that Diez's solution (rejected by Littré) is right and that *rapiere* is
for *raspiere*, a name given in contempt, meaning a rasper or poker. Hence also
a *proking-spit* of Spaine = a Spanish rapier (Nares). Cp. Span. *raspadera* a raker from
*raspar* to rasp, scrape." Skeat.

In Q° I. of Hamlet, à propos the fencing scene, we find (Dowden's Edition),
  "Mary, Sir, that yong Laertes in twelve venies  (venues = bouts or thrusts)
    At Rapier and Dagger do not get three oddes of you."

But, by the date of the following edition, the fashion had changed, foils are
introduced, and a "Bragart Gentleman" has developed into the Euphuistic "Water-
fly" Osric.

# *Prologue* 27

This Yorke is commonly regarded as a traitor for having deserted and fought on the Spanish side in the Low Countries, surrendering a fort of which he was governor near Zutphen to the enemy. Camden's account may be read in two versions, either in that of Abraham Darcie's translation from the French of P. D. B. in the 1625 edition of Camden's *Annals of Queen Elizabeth*, or in the 1688 edition of his *History of Princess Elizabeth*, and I select the former for quotation for the sake of its more vigorous English:—

"This *Yorke*, borne in *London*, was a man most negligent and lazy, but desperately hardy; he was in his time most famous among those who respected Fencing, having been the first that brought into *England* that wicked and pernicious fashion to fight in the Field in Duels, with a Rapier called a Tucke[1], onely for the thrust: the English having till that very time, used to fight with Backe-swords, slashing and cutting one the other, armed with Targets or Bucklers, with very broad weapons, accounting it not to be a manly action to fight by thrusting and stabbing, and chiefly under the waste."

As early as 1590 we find Sir John Smythe, in his *Discources on matters Militarie*, inveighing against the preference shown by "armed men Piquers" (Pikemen) who "rather weare Rapiers of a yard and a quarter long the blades or more, than strong short arming Swords and Daggers... which they cannot with any celeritie draw, if the blades of their swords be so long."

Thus it seems clear that Sir Frederick Pollock is in the right when he traces the parentage of the two-edged rapier to the "military sword of all work in the form it had assumed in the first half of the 16th century, lengthened, narrowed and more finely pointed[2]."

In introducing the fascinating and perfidious dagger, (of which the author last quoted thinks the thrusting-sword is only the extension, but I venture to submit that its etymology proves it an abbreviation from a longer weapon), I cannot deny myself the pleasure of trying to repro-

[1] "The little rapier cal'd a tucke." *Verdun.* To tucke=*trousser* (I'll "truss" or skewer you). Randle Cotgrave's Dict. 1650.
"Espée Espagnole. A Rapier or Tucke." Ibid.
[2] *The forms and history of the Sword.* Blackwood, 1883.

duce that fine piece of inlaid and polished prose, in which Paul de Saint
Victor[1] eulogises this most incisive and penetrating of weapons:

"The dagger, which is a shortened glaive, or a lengthened poignard,
was called in the 14th century *Misericord*, because, thrust at the throat
of an overthrown adversary, it forced him to ejaculate its name.    In
the 16th century, the dagger no longer goes to war; it becomes a
duelling arm—terrible and traitorous; now parrying the rapier-thrust,
anon insidiously insinuating itself into the openings of fence, to deal the
adversary a 'coup de Jarnac': sometimes the dagger, naked and smooth to
the eye, hid within itself a trident : two little lateral blades, incorporated
with the central one, bifurcated under pressure of a spring hidden in
the shoulder.    'Twas a viper protruding its triple tongue of venom."

A very different type this poignard or stiletto from the

"Long heauie Daggers, with great brauling Ale-house hilts (which were never
used but for private fraies and braules, and that within less than these fortie yeres
(i.e. 1550—1590) since which time through long peace, we have forgotten all orders
and disciplin Militarie) they doo no waies disallow, nor find fault withall, but rather
allowe them for their Souldiers to weare, than short arming Daggers of convenient
forme and substance, without hilts, or with little short crosses, of nine or ten inches
the blades, such as not onely our braue Ancestors, but al other Warlike Nations,
both in War and peace did weare, and use[2]."

In conclusion, we have to say something as to the strong attitude
which James I. took up against duels.    By constitution James was no
friend to steel and its uses; for although it may be an exaggeration
to contend that the fashion of bombastic trunks and quilted doublets
was entirely due to his ever-increasing fear of assassination, there is
reason to believe that he did not always carry out his own admonition
to his son in the *Basilikon Dōron* "to wear no ordinarie armour with
your clothes but such as is knightly and honourable; I mean rapier,

---

[1] *Anciens et Modernes*.   (Le Musée d'Artillerie.)

[2] "Certain Discources written by Sir John Smythe, Knight: concerning the formes
and effects of diuers sorts of Weapons and other verie important matters Militarie,...
and chiefly of the *Mosquet*, the *Caliver* and the *Long-bow*...and wonderful effects of
*Archers*."

swordes and daggers "—although he certainly has the sense to include fencing amongst the exercises he 'would have' him 'to use.' As early as 1612 he had allowed one of his Scottish nobles to be sentenced to death, (a sentence duly carried out,) for the murder of a fencing master; and the measure of the King's earnestness is shown in the Proclamation issued on the 13th May, 1612, offering £500 for the person of the said Lord Sanquir living or £300 for his person dead; whereas the body of Robert Carlisle, a Scottish Borderer and the instrument of murder, was assessed at £100 living or his carcase at £50, so that evidently at that time one Scottish Baron was equivalent to five or six Scottish Borderers: but something may have been added for his being a handsome fellow, and a few pounds again deducted for a "hair-scarre or cut on his lippe up to his nose, which made him snuffle in his speech," whereas the Lord Sanquir was "of a reasonable tall stature, pale-faced of a sallow colour, a small yellowish beard, one glasse or false Eie," the outcome (or the ingoing) of the rapier or dagger of the murdered man Turner. *Proclamation Book* (Record Office).

The case is reported in the State Trials as

"The arraignment and Confession of the Lord Sanquire, (who being a Baron of Scotland, was arraigned by the name of Robert Creighton Esqre) at the King's-bench Bar, in Westminster Hall, the 27th of June, for procuring the Murder of John Turner, a Master of Defence, whom he caused to be shot with a Pistol, (*cum pulvere bombardico et glandine plumbea*) by one Carliel, a Scottish-man, for thrusting out one of his Eyes in playing at Rapier and Dagger. 10 James I., A.D. 1612[1]."

Lord Sanquhar (Sanquire or Sanchar) in his defence said:

"The first motive of this fatal accident was that Turner playing with me at foils, now about seven years past at my Lord Norris's House in Oxfordshire put out one of my eyes, and that (as my Soul and Conscience was over-persuaded) willingly and of set purpose. At the taking up of the foils I protested unto him I played but as a Scholar, and not as one that would contend with a master in his own pro-fession...the order whereof...is to spare the face...I request that the king may be fairly informed of the sincerity of my confession.

*Sir Francis Bacon* (S. G.). I conceive you have sucked those affections of

[1] See Wilson's account in 2 Kennett, 688.

duelling in malice rather out of Italy and outlandish manners. His Maj^y hath shown himself God's true lieutenant and that he is no respecter of persons, but English, Scots, nobleman, fencer, (which is but an ignorant trade) are all to him alike in respect of justice."

In 1613 we have James's famous Edict against Duels (annexed to the Royal Proclamation, of which the Society of Antiquaries possesses a copy[1] and the State Paper Office none), which Isaac Disraeli declares " exhibits many proofs that it was the labour of his own hand." Indeed we have James's own word for this in his later Proclamation of 25 March 1616 "against Steelets, Pocket Daggers, Pocket Dagges and Pistols," wherein he speaks of "Our Edict proceeding from our pen" having " put down and in good part mastered that audacious custom of Duellos and challenges "; but, curiously enough, he does not include the Edict in the folio of his own works published in the same year.

The Proclamation plunges straightway into "The Slaughters which we find to haue been strangely multiplied and encreased in these later times by the boldnesse which many of Our subjects take to challenge any man into the Field." The royal remedy for "the stopping of a Vaine that bleeds both incessantly and inwardly" was that the striker should "condemn under his own hand the saucy paradox which gives liberty to gentlemen with their own swords to revenge their wrongs." He was further to promise solemnly to the Lords never to offend again, and be bound over for 6 months to good behaviour, during which time he was to be banished from the Court: and he was moreover to be subject to an action of Battery at common law: the things being "cumulative rather than privative."—We give in the Epilogue (pp. 83—85) samples of the royal argument and its expression, but it is with con-

---

[1] "A Publication of His Ma^ties Edict and Severe Censure against Private Combats...Whether within his Highnisse Dominions or without. With the Seconds, Accomplices and Adharents. Imprinted Anno 1613, at London by Robert Barker, Printer to the King's most Excellent Majestie."

I desire to express my acknowledgments to the Society for permission to make, and to Mr George Clinch, the Clerk to the Society, for his kindness in taking, the photograph of the Proclamation reproduced.

siderable logical shrewdness that James questions why Englishmen, who
had imported the fashion of duelling from foreign states, were not con-
sequent in following their precedents, which were now turned against
duels[1]. The 'Action of Battery' finds a distinct echo in the text of
the Dialogue.

But it was not merely in Proclamations and Edicts that James's
strenuous determination to eradicate the duelling propensity showed
itself. At the sitting of the Starchamber, on 26th Jan., 1615, with
a bench consisting of the Archbishop of Canterbury, the Lord Chancellor, the Lord Privy Seal, the Lord High Admiral, the Lord
Chamberlain, the Bishop of London, the Treasurer, the Comptroller
and the Vice-Chamberlain of the Household, the Lord Chief Justices of
England and the Common Pleas and the Chancellor of the Exchequer—
the grave question of a challenge to fight at single rapier, the length of
which was shown on a stick, came before the Court, which " with one
consent did utterly reject and condemn the opinion that the private duel
in any person whatsoever had any grounds of honour ; as well because
nothing can be honourable that is not lawful, and that it is no magna-
nimity or greatness of mind but a swelling and tumour of the mind
when there faileth a right and sound judgment[2]."

This case is perhaps less memorable for all the weight of intellect
upon the Bench, than for the fact that the charge was delivered by
Sir Francis Bacon, the King's Attorney General, and may be found
reported in Vol. II. of his works : and from this I extract the following
specimens of his forensic eloquence and argument :—

"......The proceedings of the great and noble commissioners martial
I honour and reverence much, and of them I speak not in any sort. But

1 In the *Recueil des Edits, Declarations, Arrests et autres pieces concernant les Duels
et Rencontres*, Paris, 1687, kindly lent me by Captain Cyril Matthey, F.S.A. (the
editor of Silver's *Paradoxes of Defence*), I find that in 1599 the French Court of
Parliament published a Judgment against Duels, followed by two edicts of the king,
Henri IV., in 1602 and 1609, a Declaration of Louis XIII. in 1611, another in 1613,
and many more in following years.

2 Cobbett's *Collection of State Trials*, Vol. II., p. 1046, "Case of Duels."

I say the compounding of quarrels, which is otherwise in use by private noblemen and gentlemen, it is so punctual, and hath such reference and respect unto the received conceits, what is before-hand, and what is behind-hand, and I cannot tell what, as without all question it doth, in a fashion, countenance and authorize this practice of duels, as if it had in it somewhat of right."

"......But, my Lords, the course which we shall take is of far greater lenity, and yet of no less efficacy; which is to punish, in this Court, all the middle acts and proceedings which tend to the duel, which I will enumerate to you anon, and so to hew and vex the root in the branches, which, no doubt, in the end will kill the root, and yet prevent the extremity of law.

......But for a difference to be made in case of killing and destroying man, upon a fore-thought purpose, between foul and fair, and as it were between single murder and vied murder, it is but a monstrous child of this latter age, and there is no shadow of it in any law divine or human.

......And of this kind was that famous example in the wars of Naples, between twelve Spaniards and twelve Italians, where the Italians bare away the victory; besides other infinite like examples worthy and laudable, sometimes by singles, sometimes by numbers.

......Therefore now to come to that which concerneth my part; I say, that by the favour of the king and the court, I will prosecute in this court in the cases following. If any man shall appoint the field, though the fight be not acted or performed. If any man shall send any challenge in writing, or any message of challenge. If any man carry or deliver any writing or message of challenge. If any man shall accept or return a challenge. If any man shall accept to be a second in a challenge of either side. If any man shall depart the realm, with intention and agreement to perform the fight beyond the seas. If any man shall revive a quarrel by any scandalous bruits or writings, contrary to a former proclamation published by his majesty in that behalf.

Nay, I hear there be some Counsel learned of Duels, that tell young men when they are before-hand, and when they are otherwise, and thereby incense and incite them to the duel, and make an art of it. I hope I shall meet with some of them too : and I am sure, my lords, this course of preventing duels is nipping them in the bud, is fuller of clemency and providence, than the suffering of them to go on, and hanging them with their wounds bleeding as they did in France[1]."

We also read in a MS. letter from John Chamberlain, preserved in the State Paper Office, dated 26th Feb. 1626, and addressed to the Rt. Hon. Sir Dudley Carleton, Bt., Ambassador to the United Provinces at the Hague :

> The King was expected at the Star Chamber, whether he went the day after the Terme (13 Feb.) and there is a case of Challenge twixt two youths of Ynnes of Court, Christmas and Bellingham, tooke occasion to make a Speach about Duells wherein he was observed to bestowe many goode words on the Spanish nation, and to gall the French more, w^ch he since interprets to be only touching that point. I heare no certaintie yet whether we shall have yt in print, the issue of all was that the gentlemen (who could say little or nothing for themselves) were fined at a 1000 £ apeece and imprisonment in the towre during pleasure.

And here, abruptly enough, breaks off my Prologue. Duels are 'violent delights,' which—sometimes—"have violent ends." How otherwise were Baudelaire's phrase, *bizarre comme le duel*, or James I.'s *Bewitching Duels* so full of felicity ?

Should any reader resent and challenge this want of ceremony, I must retain a far greater lawyer—the learned Selden—who in one of his many 'Titles of Honor'—*The Duello*—pleaded :—

---

[1] THE CHARGE OF SIR FRANCIS BACON KNIGHT, HIS Maiesties Attourney generall, touching *Duells*, vpon an informa*tion in the Star-chamber against* Priest and Wright. WITH *The Decree of the Star-chamber in* the same cause. Printed for *Robert Wilson*, and are to be sold at Graies Inne Gate, and in Paules Churchyard at the Signe *of the Bible.* 1614.

See also Spedding's *Life of Bacon*, Vol. IV., pp. 396—416, and Dalrymple's *Memorials and Letters*, (1762). Spedding did "not know where a copy of the King's Proclamation (Oct. 1613) is to be found." (See Frontispiece.)

" Reader, I open not a Fence-school, nor shall you here learn the skill of an Encounter, or advantageously in the lists to traverse your ground "—nor, I trust, the ground of my lowly Argument.

And if at all the *Manes* of Heywood become dimly conscious of a literary dwarf clambering on to the dramatic giant's shadowy shoulders; or (to shift my figure for his own) fathering upon him a base-born *Filius Populi*, let him too remember that by not signing his multifarious writings, he has become an accessory before the fact to many a later literary larceny—and also let him recall the final words of one of his own signed Prologues " Read perfectly, Examine strictly, but Censure charitably "—

> *whereof I desire*
> *To make my pen th' adoptive sire.*

I have tried to set my poor wits upon the best strops at hand, and while I dare not hope that this " Worke," even if accepted as sharpened and pointed on Heywood's whetstone, will strike out as many sparks of popularity or make as much noise in the world as the wheel of Canning's " Needy Knife-Grinder "—a *Jeu d'Esprit* of a similar temper of cultured cutlery—at least it is possible that one or two Master Grinders may appreciate the labour, (may be, the merit,) of the *Cos exsors ipsa secandi.*

A. F. S.

12 Seymour Street,
Portman Square.
*July,* 1904.

# WORKE FOR CVTLERS.

*OR,*

## A MERRY DIA-
## LOGVE BETWEENE

$\left\{ \begin{array}{l} \textit{Sword,} \\ \textit{Rapier,} \\ \textit{and} \\ \textit{Dagger.} \end{array} \right\}$

---

Acted in a Shew in the famous
*Vniuerſitie of Cambridge.*

---

---

*LONDON*
Printed by *Thomas Creede*, for *Richard Meighen* and *Thomas Iones;* and are to be sold at S. *Clements* Church without Temple-barre. 1615.

# WORKE FOR

CVTLERS : or, a merry Dialogue
betweene

$$\left\{\begin{array}{l}\textit{Sword,}\\ \textit{Rapier,}\\ \textit{and}\\ \textit{Dagger.}\end{array}\right\}$$

---

*Enter Sword.*

*Sword.*

Ay *Rapier*, come foorth, come forth I say, Ile giue thee a crowne, though it 5 be but a crackt one : what wilt not ? art fo hard to be drawne forth *Rapier ?*

*Enter*

*Enter Rapier.*

10      *Rapier.*      S'foot thou fhalt know that *Rapier*
dares enter : nay *Backe-Sword.*

*Enter Dagger, he holds Rapiers*
*hands behinde him.*

*Rapier.*   Whofe this behinde me?
*Dagger.*   Tis *Dagger* fir; what will you
neuer leaue your quarrelling?
*Rapier.*   Well *Sword, Dagger* hath defended you a good many times; but tis no matter, another time fhall serue : fhall I get
20 you out *Sword* alone, that I may haue you
*Single-fword.*
*Sword.*   Yes if youle be fingle *Rapier* too.
*Dag.*   Nay *Sword,* put the *Cafe* of *Rapiers*
afide, that there were two of them, I hope
you were able to buckle with them.
*Sword.*   Ile tell you what, if I goe into the
Field with him, hang *Sword* vp if I doe not
cut *Rapiers* poynts, and lafh him when I haue
done : nay, you fhall finde *Sword* mettle to
30 the very backe : 's foot, my teeth be an edge
at him.
*Dag.*   If you offer but to thruft towards
him

him *Rapier*, Ile ſtrike you downe.

*Sword.*  Hang him, I defie him baſe Spaniard.

*Rap.*  Defie me ? ſirrha *Sword*, *Rapier* ſpits
i' thy face : dar'ſt meete mee i' the fields, cra-
uenly Capon ?

*Sword.*  Capon ?

*Rapier.*  I Capon, ſo I ſay ſir.          40

*Dagg.*  Why any man may ſee that thou
art well caru'd *Sword*; and yet mee thinks
that *Rapier* ſhould not ſpeake of that, for it's
an hundred to one if he be not gilt too.

*Sword.*  Well *Rapier*, if thou goeſt into
the fields with me, Ile make a Capon of you
before I haue done with you, you ſhall nere
come home vncut Ile warrant you.

*Dagger.*  Nay, you ſhall finde *Sword* a
notable Cutter.          50

*Rapier.*  He a Cutter ? alas he nere went
into the fields yet, but he was ſoundly hackt
before he came out.

*Sword.*  Nere talke you of hacking, for
it's a hundred to one if you haue not the
*Foyle-Rapier*.

*Rapier.*  'S foot if you be ſo *Short-Sword*,
*Rapier* nere feares you : come a long.

*Dagger.*  Nay nere goe, for if you doe,
                                        Ile

60 Ile fende one after you, which fhall fcowre
you both.  The *Cutler* can doe it.  I haue feene
him handle you both brauely.

*Sword.*  The *Cutler*, Alas wee are the beft
Friends hee has, and if it were not for vs,
the *Cutler* might foone fhut vp his fhoppe.

*Dagger.*  Alas *Sword*, you need not talke
of his fhutting vp of Shoppe, and if it had
not beene for him, you had broken by this
time *Sword*, Nay, nere talke : For you know
70 hee can holde your nofe to the Grind-ftone,
when hee lift.

And as for you *Rapier*, you knowe hee
brought you vp firft, and if you had ftayed
with him ftill, it might haue bene better for
you.

*Rapier.*  Better for mee ?  Alas hee knewe
not how to vfe mee.

*Dagger.*  Hee vfde you too well indeede :
for when you were with him he furnifht you
80 with Siler and euery thing, but now you are
worne out of all fafhion.  You are euen like
a Lapwing, you are no fooner Hatcht *Rapier*, but you runne abroade prefently from
him.

*Rapier.*  Yet I fcorne to runne away from
him.

*Sword.*

*Sword.* But it were more wifedome then to ftand : For the *Cutler* is a man as well Armed as any man I knowe, and has as good skill ins weapons.                           90

*Rapier.* Ha *Sworde*, is the winde in that Doore ? Faith nowe I fee which waye you ftand bent *Sworde*, you had rather fleepe in a whole skinne, then goe into the Fields to trye your felfe.

*Sword.* Syr, *Sword* has been proou'd before now, and yet heele prooue himfelfe againe with you, if you dare follow him.

*Dagger.* Doe you heare *Sworde* ? If you goe, looke for *Dagger* at your backs prefent- 100 lie ; For I am a Iuftice of Peace, and am fworne to keepe and defend the Peace.

*Rapier.* Syr, wee will fight, and doe you take it in *Dudgeon Dagger* if you pleafe : if you once offer to hinder vs, Ile fo Pummell you *Dagger*, that you were neuer better Pummeld in your life ; And howfoeuer, I hope theres Lawe againft you as well as others, and *Rapier* can put vp a *Cafe* againft you.                                           110

*Dagger.* Alas I care not if you were both Plaintifes againft mee, you fhall finde *Dagger* your Defendant Ile warrant you: I, and

I, and if neede bee, I could put vp an Action
of Batterie againſt you.

*Sword.* What talke you of Law? *Sword*
ſcornes to haue any other Law then *Martialꞁ*
law, and that vpon you *Rapier.*

*Dagger.* Away *Sworde,* the Time was in-
120 deed when thou waſt a notable Swaſh-buck-
ler, but now thou art growne olde *Sword.*

*Rapier.* I, you doe well, to excuſe his
Cowardiſe.

*Sword.* Why Sir, tis well knowne that
*Sword* has flouriſht in his dayes.

*Dagger.* Flouriſht? yfaith Syr I, I haue
ſeene *Sword* hang with nothing but Scarffes
ere now.

*Rapier.* With Scarffes? with a Halter, if
130 he had beene well ſeru'de. For hees a notable Theefe. *Dagger.* A Theefe?

*Rapier.* I, a Thiefe.

Did you nere heare of *Cutting-Dicke,* this is
the very ſame man.

*Dagger.* Nay *Rapier,* nere hit *Sword* ith
teeth with that : for you know you were both
Indited for treaſon before now, and were in
danger to be hangd, and drawn too, and had
eſcapt well if you had not bene quarterd.

140      *Sword.* I hope knows how to keep his *quarters.*

*Dagger.* You are a craftie *Foxe Sword* : It

were

were well if you knewe howe to keepe your
friendſhip too, for Gentlemen and Friendes
ſhould not fall out.

    *Sword. Rapier* a Gentleman ?

    *Rap.* A Gentleman ? and has Armes.

    *Dag.* But mee thinkes *Sworde* by the very
founding of his Name ſhould bee the better
Gentleman, and has the better Armes too:
for if the truth were well knowne, *Rapier* hath 150
but one arme.

    *Rapier. Sword* beare Armes? Hees a baſe
companion. Alas I haue knowne you beare a
Basket *Sword.*

    *Dag.* If you looke ith *booke of Armorie*, Ile
warrant you, you ſhall finde *Sworde* of more
antiquitie then you *Rapier:* Hee deriues his
Pedigree from *Morglay, Beuis of South-hamp-
tons ſword*; and that from S. *George his ſword,*
that killd the Draggon.             160

    *Rapier.* I, *the draggon in Sussex*, the other
day: But Ile warrant you *Rapiers* of as good
a blood as hee for his hart.

    *Dag.* Byth maſſe, I thinke indeed, you are
both well ſanguind. Your both of one blood,
only thers this difference, that *ſword* coms of
the elder brother, & *you Rapier* of the yõger.

    *Rapier.* And oftentimes the younger bro-
ther prooues the better Souldier.

                             *Dag.*

170  *Dagger.*  Nay, *Dagger* will defende you both for good Souldiers.

*Sworde.*  *Rapier* a Souldier? When did you ere knowe *Rapier* fight a Battell?

*Dagger.*  Yes *Rapier* is a Souldier, and a Man as well Armed at all poyntes as anie one.

*Sword.*  No, no, its *Sworde* that's the notable Souldier; Why, theres none of all you Captaines could doe anie thing in Warre 180 without him.

*Rapier.*  I hope *Rapier* hath not beene at Fencing-Schoole all this while for nothing.

*Dagger.*  Alas there's none *Maifter of Defence* but *Dagger:* But yet if you fpeake of Souldiers, the'rs Bow, Bill, and Gunne, worth twenty fuch as wee are.

*Rapier.*  Indeed they fay that *Bow* has bin an olde Souldier.

*Sword.*  Yet hees not fit for a Souldier, 190 any man may bende him as hee lift.

*Rapier.*  And as for Bow-ftring, I dare vndertake to whip him my felfe.

*Sword.*  Then let mee alone to tickle *Bowes* ownes nocke yfaith.

*Dagger.*  But what fay you to *Bill?* hees a notable fturdy villaïne.

*Sword.*

*Sword.* *Bill*, Ile pay him foundly, if ere
I reach him.

*Dagger.* Its more then you can doe, Ime
affraide ; For *Bill's* a Tall-fellow ons hands, 200
and will quickly be Wood: and then theres
*Gunne*, fuch another Bouncing-fellow too.

*Rapier.* *Gunne*, Alas hees No-body : any
little Boy will make him roare.

I haue made him goe off 'oth Fieldes, a
good many times my felfe.

*Dagger.* Well, is *Gunne* No-bodie ? Ime
fure heel giue fome blowes fometimes.

*Sword.* Its' nere but when *Powder* ouer-
charges him, then indeed heel be fomewhat 210
hote oth matter.

*Rapier.* I think that *Powder* is a vile bragger, he doth nothing but cracke.

*Dagger.* Faith I knowe not what Souldier hee is, but they fay, Hees an excellent pollitician.

*Rapier,* Hee a Pollitician ?

*Dagger.* Why, hee has an excellent wit ?

*Sword.* Pifh, Its nothing but a flafh.

*Dagger.* Ime fure I can remember fince 220
he was a Parlement-man.

*Rapier.* Hee a Parlement-man : For what
Shyre ?

*Dag.*

*Dag.* Nay ber-lady, it was for the whole
Countrey.

*Sword.* I wonder they fhould chufe him :
Why he does euery thing on the fudden.

*Dag.* Oh he plottes fhrevvdly. If they had
not look't too it, Hee had vndermined the
230 vvhole parlement-houfe.

*Sword.* I but hees No-body now-adayes,
Hees blovvne vp long agoe.

*Dagger.* Well, if eyther you, or any body
elfe fhuld meete with Povvder, yet its a hundred to one, if he meete not vvith his match.

*Rapier.* Nay, you fhould let him alone
*Dagger*, and you fhould fee that *Swords'* as
notable a bragger as Povvder.  He thinks hee
fhall nere be matcht too : but hee fhall, and
240 ouer-matcht too, by *Rapier* ; I vvarrant him.
Come *Sworde*, after your long Parley, Dare
you goe into the Fieldes ?

*Sword.* Dare I ? You fhall foone fee that :
Goe, and Ile follovv you.

*Dag.* Well faide, defperate *Dicke*, *Sword*,
You may be afham'd to offer it.  You knovve
you are tvvo-handed-*Sworde*, and *Rapier* has
but one hand (vnleffe I helpe him) to do any
good vvithall, and yet youde haue him go in-
250 to the Fieldes vvith you.  Come, theres neyther of you fhall goe.  Doe not you knovve
that

that Duells are put downe?

Youle bee bound to'th Peace euer heere-after, if you ſtrike but one ſtroke. Therefore you had beſt let me decide your controuerſie for you.

*Sword.* Why, you are a backe-Friend to vs both *Dagger.*

*Dagger.* Nay, you knowe Ime equally al-lyed to you both, and therefore ſhall proue an impartiall Iudge: How ſay you, will you be rulde by me? 260

*Rapier.* Nay let him chooſe, *Rapiers* at a good poynt, whether he will or no.

*Dagger.* Why are you ſo long *Sword* before you ſpeake?

*Sworde.* Are duells put downe? Then I am forc'de to be Friends: Speake then.

*Dagger.* Then in briefe it ſhall bee thus. *Sworde*, you ſhall beare Chiefe force ith Campe, and be made Generall of the Field, to beare ſway euery where. As for you *Ra-pier*, ſince Duells are put downe, you ſhall liue quietly and peacablie heere 'ith Court, and goe euery day in Veluet: You ſhall be Frendes with euerie one, and bee on euery ones ſide, that if occaſion ſerue, and *Sworde* be absent, ſo that matters are driuē to a puſh, 270

*Rapier*

*Rapier* fhall be the onely man to performe a
280 Combate : And I my felfe will backe you
both, as occafion fhall ferue.

How fay yee, are yee content ?

*Rapier.* Wee are.

*Dagger.* Then goe before to my Houfe,
to the *Dagger* in *Cheape :* and there weele
conclude all.

*Rapier.* A *Long-Sword.*

*Exeunt, Sworde* and *Rapier.*


### Dagger.

290 *Our weapons drawne, and yet no hurt yee finde,*
*Did Dagger then defend vnto your minde ?*
*Hee that defended others not long fence,*
*At laft hee dares not ftand ins owne defence ;*
*But this hee hopes, with you it will fuffize,*
*To craue a pardon for a Schollers Prize.*


### FINIS.

# GLOSSARIAL EPILOGUE.

*(The numbers bracketed indicate the lines of the Dialogue on pp. 37—48.)*

*Crack'd Crown* (5).

"*Ingenioso.* I may chance, indeed, give the world a bloody nose, but it shall hardly give me a crack'd crown, though it gives other poets French Crowns." *The Returne from Pernassus*, or the *Scourge of Simony*, publiquely acted by the Students of St John's Cambridge, 1606.

*Pummell* (105). "The tang (or tongue of the sword), which is of many shapes...ends in the pommel or 'little apple' (*le pommeau, il pomolo, der Knauf* or *Knopf*) into which it should be made fast by rivets or screws. The object of this globe, lozenge, or oval of metal is to counterpoise the weight of the blade, to prop the ferient of the hand, and to allow of artistic ornamentation." Burton's *Book of the Sword*, p. 124. Its further object was for use like the butt-end of a musket, to "pummell" your adversary.

*Dagger at your backs* (100). It was for some time the fashion to wear the dagger hanging at the back, cf.:

> "This dagger has mista'en, for lo his house
> Lies empty on the back of Montague."
>
> *Romeo and Juliet* v. 3.

According to Nares, the rapier and dagger were usually worn side by side.

> "His sword a dagger had, his page,
> That was but little for his age:
> It was a serviceable dudgeon
> Either for fighting, or for drudging:
> When it had stabb'd, or broke a head,
> It would scrape trenchers, or chip bread."
>
> *Hudibras* I. I. 375.

Also:

> "Thou must wear thy sword by thy side,
> And thy dagger handsumly at thy back."
>
> *The longer thou livest &c.*, 1570.

<u>Dudgeon</u> (104). See Nares's "Glossary." A peculiar kind of handle to a dagger, made of the root of box—the *Cambridge Dictionary* of 1693 has "A dudgeon-haft—manubrium appiatum or buxeum"; see too Gerard's *Herbal*, in Johnson's edition, under *Box-Tree*: "Turners and Cutlers...doe call this wood *dudgeon*, wherewith they make *dudgeon-hafted* daggers." Also *Macbeth* II. I:

> "I see thee still,
> And on thy blade and dudgeon, gouts of blood."

Beaumont and Fletcher's *Coxcomb* V. I:

"A dudgeon-dagger will serve him to mow down sin withal."

1611. "Dague a roëlles—a Scottish Dagger—a Dudgeon haft dagger. Cotgrave." (Murray.)

The root of the box-tree was also called *dudgeon* from being curiously marked, "the root (of box) is dudgin or full of work." Holland's Pliny B. XVI. c. 16.        (Skeat.)

Evelyn does not mention the dudgeon haft, but speaking of *Beech* he says: "Of the thin *Lamina* or *Scale* of this wood (as our Cutlers call it) are made *Scabards* for Swords."        *Sylva*, chap. V. 2.

Mr Guy Francis Laking writes to me *à propos* of the hilts of the daggers (nos. 1324 and 1334) in the Wallace Collection " To the best of my belief the grips of the daggers you name in the Wallace Collection are of box-wood."

*Francis Junius* in his *Etymologicum Anglicanum* (ed. by Lye, Oxon. 1743) has the following:

"*Dudgeon haft*. Manubrium apiatum [Dudgeon, Pugiuncula à Teut. Dolch Pugio q.d. Dolkin vel à Degen, Gladius. Skin.]."

*Pugio*, a dagger, hence It. *pugnale*, Fr. *poignard*.

"O plumbeum pugionem." O leaden dagger, *i.e.* O weak argument. Cicero.

1380. *Ordinance for Cutlers.* "Lond. in Letter Book H.—cf. cxviii., 'Qe nulles manches darbre forsqe *digeoñ* soyent colourez' (tr. in Riley, *Mem. London*, 1868), see Arnold's *Chronic.* (1811), 245." Murray's Dictionary.

1687. "With Dudgeon Dagger at his back" (Cotton's Poet. Works).

*Dagger.*

1375. Fragm. Vetusta xxiv. in Sc. Acts (1844).

"Habeat equum...ensem et cultellum qui dicitur *dagare.*"

1562. See Act 5 Eliz. c. 7, § 3 as to "Dagger-blades, handles" &c. "The Devil may buy us even dagger-cheap."

Bishop Andrews' Sermon.

> "The stilleto-beard, oh! it makes me afeard,
> It is so sharp beneath,
> For he that doth place a dagger in's face
> What wears he in his sheath?"
>
> *The Ballad of the Beard.*

*Le Prince d'Amour*, 1660. ? Earlier than Charles I. *Satirical Songs and Poems on Costume*, F. W. Fairholt (Percy Soc.), 1849. See pamphlet by J. A. Repton, F.S.A.

1592. "All you that will not...weare ale-house daggers at your backes." Nashe, *P. Penilesse* (Shaks. Soc.), 40.

*Dagger-Ale* and *Dagger vein-piercing.* "I will stab him that will not pledge your health, and with a dagger pierce a vein to drink a full health to you" (see note 39 to *Honest Whore*).

"From stabbing of arms, flap-dragons &c. good Mercury defend us." *Cynthia's Revels*, Act v. Sc. 2.

*Backsword* (11). A sword with only one cutting edge.

1611. Cotgrave. "*Badelaire*, a short and broad Back Sword."

1750. Bolingbroke. *Pol. Tracts*, 214. "The backsword of Justice which cuts only on one side."

2. A stick with a basket-hilt used instead of a sword in fencing, a single-stick.

1699. "I'm much in love with fencing, but, I think, backsword is the best play."          Farquhar, *Love and a Bottle*, 1728.

1672. "To the Back-Swords of London."

Davenant, *Siege of Rhodes*.

1597. "I knew him a good Back-Swordsman."

2 *Henry IV*. III. 2. 70.

1857. "The great times for back-swording."

Hughes, *Tom Brown*.
(Murray's *New English Dictionary*, 1888.)

"The chief modern varieties of the curved blade are the Broadsword, the Backsword, the Hanger and the Cutlass, the Scymitar and Düsack, the Yataghan and the Flissa."

Burton's *Book of the Sword*, p. 123.

*Vide* Egerton Castle's *Schools and Masters of Fence*, chap. XIII., and Captain Hutton's *The Sword and the Centuries*, chap. XXVI., for full historical accounts of "back-swording."

"His metamorphosis behold
From Glasgow frieze to cloth of gold;
His back-sword, with the iron hilt,
To rapier, fairly hatch'd and gilt."

*The Reformation.*
(Quoted by Scott in *Fortunes of Nigel.*)

"Yet I confesse, in old times, when blowes were only used with short Swords and Bucklers and back Sword, these kind of fights were good and most manly, but now in these daies fight is altered."

Silver's *Paradoxes of Defence*, 1599.

*Single-Sword : Single Rapier* (21). "At the Single Sword, Sword and Dagger and Sword and Buckler, they forbid the thrust, and at the single Rapier and Rapier and Dagger they forbid the blow" (*i.e.* cut).

...If the thrust be best why do we not use it at the single Sword... If the blow be best, why do we not, use it at the single Rapier, Rapier and Poingard?" *Ibid.*

*Raper.* Philip Stubbes in *The Anatomie of Abuses* says "Swordes Daggers and *rapers* of bare iron and steel were as handsome as they, and much more conducive to that ende whereto swordes and *rapiers* should serve."

The Buckinghamshire Rapers originally spelt their name Rapier.
*Memoirs of a Highland Lady.*

<u>*Case of Rapiers*</u> (23). "The case of Swords as it was termed in England, implied a right and left handed sword that were worn together in the same Scabbard. Giacomo di Grazzi, the Fencing Master, writing in 1570 speaks of their use with enthusiasm. The fight with the case of Swords much resembled that of the Sword and Dagger, with the exception that the longer weapon in the left hand made its action more offensive. It was taught by the Masters Agrippa and Marozzo in the middle of the 16th Century."

Guy Francis Laking, F.S.A., *Catalogue of Armour in Wallace Collection*, and Egerton Castle and Captain Hutton *passim.*

<u>*Rapier and Dagger*.</u> "I have seen it disallowed that a gentleman chalenged to fight with rapier and dagger should present himselfe in the equipage of a man at Armes; or that another should offer to come with his cloake instead of a dagger." Florio's Montaigne, II. 26.

<u>*Rapiers at a good poynt*</u> (263). "But whan a man perceiveth that he is entred so farre that hee can not drawe backe without a burdeyne, hee muste, bothe in suche thinges he hath to doe before the combat and also in the combat be utterlye resolved with hymselfe, and always shewe a readineses and a stomake[1]. And not as some dooe, passe the matter in arguing and *pointes*[2], and having the choise of weapon, take suche as

---

[1] Surely the origin of Polonius's
 " Beware of entrance to a quarrel" etc.

[2] An unconscious pun, like Rapier's intentional one.

have neyther poynte nor edge[1]. And arme themselves as thoughe they shoulde goe against the shotte of a Cannon."

*The Courtier* (Sir T. Hoby's Translation).

"Let us be at a poynt what is best to be done."

*Macbeth* IV. 3. 135.

*Buckle* (25)=engage in close fight: Shakespeare, 1 *Henry VI*. I. 2. 95; v. 3. 28 *too strong for me to buckle with*, IV. 4. 5; 3 *Henry VI*. I. 4. 50.

"*Lambert.* And, Serlsby, I have there a lusty boy,
That dares at weapon buckle with thy son."

*Friar Bacon and Friar Bungay*, Sc. XIII.

*Cut Rapiers poynts* (28) and *Points*. "Foresleves of velvet, called in those days poignettinge of a doublette." *Institucion of a Gentleman*.

"Then he brought him to a Mercers shop, and said to the Mercer let me see of your best silken pointes, the Mercer did presently show him some of seaven groates a dozen...then he said to the Maister of Defence, there is one dozen for you, and here is another for me."

Silver's *Paradoxes*.

"Laces or ties frequently having ornamental tags and as often used in the 16th and 17th centuries, so profusely employed to secure different parts of dress, as to form a trimming, sometimes to make quite a fringe."

Draper's Dictionary.

Like their supersessors, pins, they were chiefly manufactured at Bristol, "Bristowles great trade is the making of points, and that was the chief mystery that was exercised in the town."

Stafford, *Compendious Examination &c.*, 1581.

Shakespeare also puns upon the word in *Twelfth Night*—

"*Clown.* But I am resolved on two points.

*Mar.* That if one break, the other will hold; or if both break your gaskins will fall."

"Truss my points, Sir." *Eastward Hoe*, 1605.

[1] Cp. Cyrano de Bergerac's thoroughly gallant, euthanasian and Mercutian maxim :
"Mourir la pointe au cœur, en même temps qu'aux lèvres." Rostand.

# Glossarial Epilogue 55

*Lash* (28). "Ouerlashing in apparel is so common a fault, that the very hyerlings of some of our Players, jet under gentlemen's noses in sutes of silke" &c.    Stephen Gosson, *School of Abuse*, 1579.

*'S foot* (10 and 57). "One sware me God from top to toe with one breath...the other...sware me by the flesh of God, that if swearing were to help him but one ace, he would not leave one piece of God unsworn, neither within nor without."    Ascham's *Toxophilus*.

"I know a man that will never swear but by *Cock and pye*, or *mouse-foot*. I hope you will not say these be oaths."
*The Plaine Man's Pathway to Heaven.* By Arthur Dent 1601.

"By the Mouse-foot, some give him hard words."
    T. Heywood's *First Part of K. Edward the Fourth.*

"This infamous custom of Swearing I observe reigns in England lately more than any where else; though a *German* in highest puff of passions swears a *hundred thousand Sacraments*, the *Italian* by the *W...e of God*, the *French* by his *Death*, the *Spaniard* by his *Flesh*, the *Welshman* by his *Sweat*, the *Irishman* by his *Five Wounds*, though the *Scot* commonly bids the *Devil hale his soul*; yet for variety of Oaths the English Roarer puts down all."    James Howell, *Familiar Letters*, Aug. 1, 1628.

We here see the origin of three of the oaths familiar on the stage, viz. *'s foot*, *od's Fish* (Charles II.) and *Zounds*, are clearly "God's foot," "God's Flesh" ("How art thou Fishified!"), and "God's Wounds."

"God's body, God's body, my Lord Chancellor (Sir Thomas More), a parish clerk, a parish clerk!"    Roper's *Life of Sir Thomas More.*

The Duke of Norfolk used "vain repetitions, as the Heathen do."

"*Dick Bowyer.* 's hart, and I lye, call me Jebuzite.

*Peter.* Bowyer a Captayne? a Capon, a button mould, a lame haberdine (salt cod), a red-beard Sprat, a Yellow-hammer...a very Jackdaw with his toung slit.

*Bowyer.* Zounds, what a Philistine is this."
    *The Tryall of Chevalry.*

Jeremy Collier in his *Short view of the Immorality and Profaneness of the English Stage* (4th ed. 1699) has this upon 'Commuted' Oaths:

"Sometimes they mince the matter; change the Letter, and keep the Sense, as if they had a mind to steal a Swearing, and break the Commandment without Sin.   At another time, the Oaths are clipt but not so much within the Ring, but that the *Image and Superscription* are visible...*Shakespeare* is comparatively sober, *Ben Johnson* is still more regular; And as for *Beaumont* and *Fletcher* in their Plays, they are commonly Profligate Persons that Swear, and even those are reprov'd for it."

There seems no doubt that much of the mincing and "clipping" of oaths such as "'*s foot*" etc. was due to the Statute against Swearing (3 Jac. I. c. 21) "for the preventing and avoiding of the great abuse of the holy Name of God in Stage-plays, Enterludes etc." which enacted a forfeit of £10 for each offence.

*Base Spaniard* (34).    Cf. Ben Jonson's *The New Inn*, Act ii., Sc. v.

"*Tip.*   Your *Spanish* Host is never seen in *Cuerpo*,
        Without his Paramento's Cloak and Sword.
*Fly.*    Sir, he has the Father
        Of Swords, within a long Sword : Blade *cornish* stil'd of Sir *Rud*
             *Hughdebras.*
*Tip.*   And with a long Sword, bully Bird, thy sence?
*Fly.*    To note him a tall Man, and the Master of Fence.
*Tip.*   But doth he teach the *Spanish* way of *Don Lewis*?
*Fly.*    No, the Greek Master he.
*Tip.*   What call you him?   *Fly.*   Euclid.
*Tip.*   Gi' me the Moderns.   *Fly.*   Sir, he minds no Moderns,
        Go by, Hieronimo !   *Tip.*   What was he?   *Fly.*   The Italian
        That plaid with Abbot *Antony* i' the Fryers,
        And *Blinkin-sops* the bold.   *Tip.*   I' marry, those
        Had Fencing Names, what's become o' them?
*Host.*  They had their times, and we too say, they were.
        So had *Caranza* his : so had *Don Lewis,* &c."

See also Act iv. Sc. 2, passim.

"Don Lewis of Madrid is the sole Master now of the World."

"A dainty spruce Spaniard, with hair black as jet,
Long Cloak with round Cape, a long rapier and poignard....
A haughty high German of Hamborough town,
A proper tall gallant, with mighty mustachoes,
He weeps if the lass upon him do but frown;
Yet he's a great fencer, that comes to o'ermatch us.
But yet all his fine fencing could not get the lass &c."

> *Blew-Cap for me*, see Evans' *Old Ballads*,
> vol. III. p. 255, from a black letter copy
> printed by T. Lambert.

> F. W. Fairholt, *Songs and poems on Costume*.
> Percy Society (24, 1849).

*Spaniard* (34). "We like degenerate sonnes, haue forsaken our fore-fathers vertues with their weapons, and haue lusted like men sicke of a strange ague, after the strange vices and deuises of Italian French and Spanish Fencers."     G. Silver's *Paradoxes of Defence* (1599).

"This is the maner of Spanish fight, they stand as braue as they can with their bodies straight upright, narrow spaced, with their feet continually mouing, as if they were in a dance, holding forth their armes and Rapiers verie straight against the face or bodies of their enemies: and this is the only lying to accomplish that kind of fight."
                                                                    *Ibid.*

*Spanish and French Duellist.* "Your *French-man* is much the fairer *Duellist*, for when hee goeth to the *Field*, he commonly puts off his doublet and opens his breast; the *Spaniard* cleane contrary, besides his shirt, hath his doublet quilted, his coat of maile, his cassock, and strives to make himself impenetrable."
          James Howell's *Instructions for Forraine Travell.*   1642.

"Place three Frenchmen in the deserts of Libya, and they will never live one moneth together without brawling, falling out and scratching one another."     Florio's Montaigne II. 27.

*Enter the Englishman and Spaniard.*

*Spa.* The wall, the wall!

*Eng.* 'Sblood! Spaniard, you get no wall here, unless you would have your head and the wall knocked together.

*Spa.* Signor Cavaliero d'Ingleterra, I must have the wall.

*Eng.* I do protest, hadst thou not enforced it, I had not regarded it; but, since you will needs have the wall, I'll take the pains to thrust you into the kennel.

*Spa.* Oh, base Cavaliero. My sword and poinard, well-tried Toledo, shall give thee the imbrocado.

*Eng.* Marry, and welcome, sir, come on.

(They fight: he hurts the Spaniard.

*Spa.* Holo, holo! thou hast given me the canvisado.

*Eng.* Come, sir; will you any more?

*Spa.* Signor Cavaliero, look behind thee. A blade of Toledo is drawn against thee.

(He looks back: he kills him.

Thomas Heywood's *If you know not me you know nobody, or The troubles of Queen Elizabeth*, 1605, ed. by J. P. Collier.

*Short Sword* (57). "If we will have this true Defence, we must seeke it where it is, in short Swords, short Staues, the halfe Pike, Partisans, Glaues (Glaives) or such like weapons of perfect lĕgths, not in long Swords, long Rapiers, nor frog pricking Poiniards."

Silver's *Paradoxes of Defence* (Matthey's edition).

*Gilt* (44). (*Equivoque* gelt.) "To these haue they their rapiers, swordes, and daggers, gilt twise or thrise ouer the hiltes with good angell golde, or else argented ouer with Siluer both within and without; and if it be true, as I heare say it is there be some hiltes made all of pure siluer it selfe, and couered with golde. Othersome at the least are damasked (damascened) varnished and ingrauen meruilous goodly; and least any thing shoulde be wanting to set forth their pride, their scaberdes and sheathes are of velvet, or the like; for leather, thoughe it'se more profitable and as seemely, yet wil it not carie such a porte or countenaunce as the other."

P. Stubbes, *Anatomie of Abuses* (ed. Wm B. D. D. Turnbull, F.S.A.S., Pickering 1836, from the 3rd edition 1585).

T. Lionell, *A Capon*. Reginald, *Geld the Rascall*. Heywood's *The English Traveller*.

*Scower (Scowre)* (60). "O' my conscience this Morning I beat twenty Higling-Women, spread their butter about the Kennel, broke all their Eggs, let their sucking Pigs loose, flung down all the Peds with Pippins about the Streets, scower'd like Lightning, and kick'd Fellows like Thunder: ha, ha, ha." Shadwell's *Scowrers*, Act IV. Sc. I.

"But it becommethe a gentleman (saye they) to be a Royster, whyche worde I doe not well understand onles it signifie a ruffian... And if sundrye things myght haue one name, then myghte a hatchet bee called a spade...for if a Gentleman haue in hym any humble behauour then Roysters do cal suche one by the name of a Loute, a Clynchepope, or one that knoweth no facions."

"A Ruffian and an unquiet man, geuen to quarels, such one as we cal a Roister."
             *The Institucion of a Gentleman* 1568 (reprint 1839).

In one of Marston's satires, *Reactio* (printed with his *Pigmalion's Image*, 1598), upon Bishop Joseph Hall, himself one of the earliest (if not the first after Skelton) and greatest of English satirists, we find

> "Come, manumit thy *plumy pinion*,
>      *And scower the sword of elvish champion*."

The words in italics are said by Hall's editor T. W. Singer (1824) to be a paraphrase of Hall's own words in *A Defiance to Envy*. (Marston was Hall's Cambridge rival.)

> "*Ralph.* 'I'll scour you for a goblet.' A slang term for chastise.
>             Dr A. W. Ward's *Dr Faustus*.
> 'I'll scour you with my rapier.'
>             Nym to Pistol. *Hy. V.* II. I. 60."

The *Scourers* were the "Mohocks" or "Rufflers" of their day. Their name forms the title of one of Shadwell's plays, wherein an old rake thus boasts of his early exploits—"I knew the Hectors, and before

them the Muses, and the Tityretu's; they were brave Fellows indeed !
In these days, a man could not go from the Rose Garden to the Piazza
once, but he must venture his life twice, my dear Sir Willie."
Scott's note to *The Fortunes of Nigel.*

"The bravo of the Queen's day...had, since the commencement
of the Low Country wars, given way to a race of Sworders, who used
the rapier and dagger instead of the far less dangerous sword and
buckler." Introduction to *F. of N.*

"Duels in every street were maintained: divers sects and peculiar
titles passed unpunished and unregarded, as the sect of The Roaring Boys,
Bonaventers, Bravadors, Quarterors and such like."
History of the First Fourteen Years of King James's Reign.<br>*Somers's Tracts*, ed. by W. Scott, vol. II. p. 266.

Sir Thomas Overbury has the "Character" of "A Roaring Boy."

"*Iudicio.* Methinks he is a ruffian in his style
Withouten bands or garter's ornament:
He quaffs a cup of Frenchman's Helicon
Then roister doister in his oily terms
Cuts, thrusts and foins at whomsoever he meets."
*The Returne from Pernassus* 1606 :<br>first acted at St John's College Cambridge 1604.

*Broken by this time, Sword* (68). The *Equivoque* may partly turn
upon the recollection of the Sword-Breakers (*brise-épées*) mostly of the
fifteenth century, of which Sir R. Burton gives four illustrations on
p. 138 of his *Book of the Sword*. They were made with a toothed or
indented edge, found in Arab, Indian and other Eastern weapons. (See
Wallace Collection.)

*Furnisht you with Siler* (80). See Note to *Gilt*, p. 58.

*Fashion* (81). "Fencing (Right honorable) in this new fangled age,
is like our fashions, euerie daye a change, resembling the Cameleon, who

altereth him selfe into all colours saue white : so Fencing changeth into all wards saue the right."

George Silver, *Paradoxes of Defence*, 1599.

*Silver* (80).

"A *Gull* is he which while he proudly weares
*A silver-hilted* rapier by his side,
Indures the lyes and knocks about the eares
Whilst in his sheath his sleeping sword doth bide."

Sir John Davies's Epigram.

*Lapwing* (82).  "This Lapwing runs away with the shell on his head."
*Hamlet*, v. 2.

"As the Lapwing runneth away with the shell on her head, as soon as she is hatched."
Mere's *Wit's Treasury*.

*Hatcht* (82).  "Hatching" was the term for engraving and inlaying the hilts of weapons : and still survives as a technical term of engraving.

"His rapier and dagger richly hatcht with gold."

*You stand bent* Sworde (93).  "As the sword of the best tempered metal is most flexible, so the truly generous are most pliant and courteous in their behaviour to their inferiors."

Thos. Fuller, *The holy State* (The True Gentleman).

See Shakespeare, *Much Ado*, II. 3. 232, IV. I. 188. *Twelfth Night*, II. 4. 38. *Hamlet*, II. 2. 30, III. 2. 401.

*Is the Winde in that door* (91) or, as we now say, "Sits the wind in that quarter?" Cf. Gifford's note to "Is the wind there" in Ben Jonson's *Bartholomew Fair* :—"A proverbial expression. 'Is it so?' 'Have I found you out?'"

"*Philologe.*  What handling belongeth to the weather?
*Toxophilus.*  Knowing of his wind with him, against him, side wind, full side wind, side wind quarter with him, side wind quarter against him and so forth."
Ascham.

*Scarf* (127).   "First mentioned as an article of dress in the time of Elizabeth."                    Draper's Dictionary.

"Then must they haue their silk scarfs cast about their faces, and fluttering in the wind with great lapels at every end, either of gold or silver or silk, which they say they wear to keep them from sun-burning."
                    Stubbes, *Anatomie of Abuses.*

"The scarfed bark," *Merch. of Venice.*

*Cutting-Dicke* (133) seems to have been a lost play by Heywood.

F. G. Fleay (*Biographical Chronicle of the English Drama* 1559—1642, vol. I., p. 290) has this entry : " 1602, Sep. 2.   Additions to *Cutting Dick* £1.   This play must have been written before Worcester's men joined Henslow."   Also in his *History of the Stage* (1559—1642) p. 155.   "Cutting Dick, i.e. Dick Bowyer, the same as *The Trial of Chivalry*" (by Heywood and another), i.e. *The History of the Tryall of Chevalry with the Life and Death of Cavallero Dick Bowyer*, 1604, reprinted in Bullen's *Old Plays.*

*Cutting Dick*, so "*Val. Cutting*—a Roarer or Bully," one of the dramatis personae in *Bartholomew Fair.*

Cf. also Stephen Gosson's *The Schoole of Abuse* (1579, ed. Arber). "The skil of Logicians is exercysed in caueling, the cunning of Fencers applied to quarrelling: they thinke themselues no Scholers, if they bee not able to finde out a knotte in every rushe;...Every Duns will be a Carper, every *Dick* Swash a common *Cutter*."   (Here Duns may be *Duns* Scotus or *Dunce*, and Dick Swash may be the original of our Cutting-Dicke.)

*Cutting* and *Cutter* (50).   "A certain Justice of Peace with a swaggering companion called Cutting Tom, who in a braverie took the wall of Mr Justice."
          *Jack of Dover* (from a copy in Bodleian Library), 1604,
          Wm Firebrand, Percy Society, Vol. VII.

Gabriel Harvey in his "*Foure Letters and Certain Sonnets, especially touching Robert Greene*" (1592) makes one of his accusations, "his employnge of Ball (surnamed Cuttinge Ball) till he was intercepted at Tiborne."

Cf. Cowley's *Cutter of Coleman Street.*

"*Cutter*" signifies swaggering bully : a cutpurse (A. W. Ward). See *How a man may Choose a Good Wife from a Bad*, Act v. Sc. 1: "Sir, do you not pink doublets?...I took you for a Cutter, you are of a great Kindred."—Roger North, in his *Lives of the Norths*, vol. II. p. 57 (ed. 1826), says of Laurence Hyde, Earl of Rochester (the "Lory" of Dryden's *The Young Statesmen*), that one of his infirmities was "passion, in which he would swear like a cutter." (A. W. Ward's *History of English Dramatic Literature*, vol. III. ch. IX. p. 327 note.) It would be an interesting sociological problem to trace the evolution of "cutting" through literature down to its modern sense. Cf. *The Art of Cutting* (early 19th century).

<u>*Haue not the Foyle*</u> (56). So in Ben Jonson's *Discoveries*, where he says "the multitude commend Writers, as they do Fencers, who if they come in robustiously...are received for the *Braver-fellows*...when a slight touch of their Adversary gives all that boisterous Force, *the foil*."

"The fame of a gentleman that carieth weapon, yf it once take a foile in any little point through dastardlines or any other reproche, doeth evermore continue shameful in the worlde."

> *The Courtier*, Sir T. Hoby, 1561.

"*Emperor*. Bestir thee Jaques, take not now the foil
> Lest thou dost lose what foretime thou didst gain."
>> *Friar Bacon and Friar Bungay*, Sc. IX.

Also *I Henry VI.* v. 3. 23.

To foil is from the O.Fr. *affoler*, Ital. *affollare* to press hard.

> A. W. Ward, Note to *Friar Bacon and Friar Bungay*.

"But gentle thoughts when they may *give the foyle*
> Save them that yield, and spare where they may spoil."
>> Prologue to *Woman Kilde with Kindnesse*. 3rd edition 1617.

<u>*Foxe*</u> (141). "The wolf-mark of the Passau sword-smiths was borrowed from the city arms, which consist of 'Or, a wolf figure,

statant gardant.'   Later, and especially in the 16th century, this mark
was adopted in other places, and especially by Solingen smiths.   These
blades were known as 'foxes,' in England, doubtless from the 'wolf'
inscription."

> R. C. Clephan, *The Defensive Armour and Weapons and*
> *Engines of War &c.*, p. 172.

"Passau and Solingen were celebrated at a very early time for
making blades of weapons, the quality of which was as highly esteemed
as those of Toledo....Another very usual mark is a wolf, which is
believed to have been granted by the Archduke Albert in 1349 to the
Armourers' Guild of Passau: it is also to be seen on some of the
earlier arms made at Solingen, in which city the armourers Clement
Horn and Johann Stopp flourished at the commencement of the
sixteenth century."

> Auguste Demmin, *History of Arms and Armour*, Bohn, p. 548.

A reproduction of the wolf-badge is given by Demmin, p. 551.
Those who have seen the rude outline of the wolf in question will
easily understand its metamorphosis into an English fox.

*Fox* (141).   "No more truth in thee than in a drawn fox," 1 *Henry
IV.*, III. 3. 129.   Dyce's *Glossary* (1902) misses the double meaning.

(Nares)           "O what blade is it,
> A Toledo or an English Fox?
> Old foxes are good blades."
> Browne, *English Moor* II. 2, Webster's *White Devil* VI. 370.

*Defendant* (113).   A word now passed into the peaceful lists of
the law-court, but quite common amongst the Elizabethans, as e.g.:
> "All which arriv'd at the evenest piece of earth
> The field afforded, the three challengers
> Turn'd head, drew all their rapiers and stood rank'd.
> When face to face the three *defendants* met them,
> Alike prepar'd, and resolute alike.
> George Chapman, *Bussy D'Ambois.*

*Action of Battery* (114). "Assault and Battery be for the most part an accomplishment of that which menace did threaten, and a performance by deedes of which the other fore-warned by words, that is to say, a violent and forcible abusing, or attempting to abuse by blowes and stripes the person of another, contrary to the peace of the realme...the law hath devised a quiet and peaceable course, to reduce him again to order, in punishing him by an action of Trespass of Assault and Batterie, wherein being convicted, hee shall satisfie the party grieved his damages and pay to the King a fine, and his bodie shall be committed to prison untill hee hath satisfied it."

Pulton's *De Pace Regis et Regni* 1623 (Black Letter).

*Martial Law* (117). See Edict against Duels (in Prologue p. 83 and *post*).

*Swash-buckler* or *Swinge-buckler* (120).

"He has ne'er a sword and buckler-man in his Fair."

Induction to *Bartholomew Fair*.

*Swash-buckler.* "A vain-glorious Sword-player or Fencer; a meer Braggadochoe, a vapouring fellow."

*To swash*, "to make fly about; to clash, or make a noise with Swords." Ed. Phillips' *New World of Words*, 1657.

"To Swash it in apparell."

Antony Wood, 1. 423 (ed. 1706). (A. Clark.)

*Basket-Sword* (154). The basket-hilt was first introduced in the Venetian Schiavona for the Schiavoni or Doge's guards of the sixteenth century. R. C. Clephan writes : " Scottish broadswords with practically this hilt... are often erroneously called 'claymores,' while, as a matter of fact, the Scottish weapon so called was a long two-handed sword, with quillons usually bending diagonally upwards,...and it is considered questionable by some authorities whether any basket hilted sword whatever was in general use in Scotland long before the 18th century began."

*Basket Hilts* is the name of one of the characters in Ben Jonson's *Tale of a Tub*, and *Puppy* meeting him in "The Fields near Pancras," and retorting upon a threat of his "school-dagger 'bout your costard," says:—"Tie up your brended bitch there, your dun rusty, Pannier-hilt poniard."

*Basket-Sword* (154). "What would you have sister, of a fellow that knows nothing but a basket-hilt and an old fox in it?"

Ben Jonson, *Bartholomew Fair* II. 6.

(See note on *Fox*, p. 64.)

"...as flat as a basket-hilt dagger."

Nat. Field, *Amends for Ladies.*

*Basket hilt* is one of the characters in John Cooke's *Greenes Tu Quoque or the Cittie Gallant*, published by his friend Thos. Heywood, 1614, 4°.

*Morglay* (158). "It is the most fortunate weapon that ever rid on poor gentleman's thigh. Shall I tell you, Sir? You talk of Morglay, Excalibur, Durindana, or so; but!...this a Toledo! Pish!...A Fleming, by heaven! I'll buy them for a guilder apiece."

Captain Bobadil; Ben Jonson, *Every Man In His Humour*, Act III. Sc. 2.

"The name *Morglay* was often given to a sword in general. Mr D. P. Fry suggests that *mor-glay* is merely an inverted form of *Clay-more*, the Celtic for *big sword*."

H. B. Wheatley (note to *Every Man In His Humour*).

"And how fair Iosian gave him (Sir Bevis) Arundel his steed
And Morgley his good Sword."          Drayton's *Polyolbion.*

*Beuis of Southampton* (158). For this famous Romance see Ellis's *Specimens* and the Publications of the Early English Text Society. "There is as much difference betwixt these two kind of fights, as there is betwixt the true picture of Sir *Beuis* of *Southampton* and Sir *Beuis* himself, if he were living."          Silver's *Paradoxes.*

*The Draggon in Sussex, the other day* (161) refers to "A strange and monstrous Serpent or Dragon," the subject of a pamphlet by A. R.

(printed at London, by John Trundle, 1614, and reprinted by Mr Charles Hindley in *The Old Book Collectors' Miscellany*, vol. II.) describing the appearance "in Sussex, two miles from Horsam, in a Woode called 'St Leonard's Forrest,'" August 1614, of a serpent "reputed to be nine feet, or rather more, in length and shaped almost in the form of an axle tree of a cart, a quantity of thickness in the midst, and somewhat smaller at both ends....He will cast his venom about four rod from him, as by woful experience it was proved on the bodies of a man and woman coming that way, who afterwards were found dead, being poisoned and very much swelled, but not preyed upon." The story is certified by John Steele and Christopher Holder, and the carrier of Horsham, who lieth at the White Horse, in Southwark, but they do not disclose the name of the Sussex St George.

<u>*Gentleman*</u>. *Arms* (149). *The Booke of Armorie* (155). I have looked through Dame Juliana Berners' (Bernes or Barnes) "ryght noble Treatise of the Lygnage of Cot Armour" (1496), John Ferne's *Blazon of Gentrie* (1586), W. Wyrley's *True Use of Armory* (1592), John Guillim's *Display of Heraldrie* (1610), Robert Glover's *Catalogue of Honour* (1610), and Edmund Bolton's *Elements of Armory* (1610), and am inclined to believe that Gerard Legh's *The Accedens of Armory* (1562) is the Booke of Armorie referred to in the text—unless it be the 1595 edition of *The Book of St. Albans* revised and much altered by Gervase Markham and re-issued as *The Gentleman's Academie &c.* 4°. At any rate the following excerpts from Legh are "germane to the matter" of "the better Gentleman"—since he differentiates nine "genera":—

*There are nine gentlemen of sundry callinges.......The first is a gentleman of auncestrie, which must nedes be a gentlemã of blood. But if he dye withoute issue, the whole cote armour is loft,......The second, is a gētleman of blood, and not of auncestry. As, when he is the secounde in degree, discended from the first of that name. The third is a gentleman of cote armour, and not of blood. That is to saye, a gentleman of cote armour of the kinges badge, as the kinges deuise geuen hym by an Herehaughte.......The fourth is alfo a gētlemã of cote armour, and not of blood, as this. The king geueth a lordſhip by patent, to him and his heyres for euer. He may beare the cote of that lordſhip.......The fift, is a yeoman, a chriſtian man. If he (I say) in the ſeruice of god and his prince, kill an heathen gentleman, of what degree ſoeuer he be (a knight baneret excepte) he ſhall beare the armes, and vſe his atchieuemẽt without any differẽce, ſauĩg only ŷ word of ŷ ſame miſcreant gẽtlemã.......The ſixt is, if a king do make a yeomã a knight, he is thẽ as a gẽtleman of blood, by ŷ royaltie of ŷ king, and knighthod. The ſeuẽth, is a gẽtleman ſpirituall. This, if he be a chorles ſõne, and is aduaũced to any ſpiritual dignitie, he is thẽ a gẽtlemã, but not of blud. But if he be a doctor of ŷ Ciuil lawe, he is a gẽtlemã as of blood, and his cote is perfit at ŷ firſt bearing. The eight, is called a gentlemã vntrial, and ſuch is he, as being brought vp in an Abbey, or wᵗ a biſſhop.......The nynth, hath ben of olde called a gentilmã Appocrifate. This is ſuche a one, as ſerueth a prince. And at his begyn-nyng, is a page, and groweth vp by his diligence, to be a grome, and ſo hyer.*

"There was never gentleman nor churle ordained but hee had father and mother: Adam and Eve, had neither father nor mother and therefore in the Sonnes of Adam and Eve first issued one both gentleman and churle...."

(Noah to his son Japhet):

"Adams Sonne, I make thee a gentleman, and thy renoune shall streth through the west part of the world...and thy dominion shall be called Asia, which is the countrie of gentlemen....From the of-spring of gentlemanly Japhet came Abraham, Moyses, Aaron and the Prophets and also the king of the right line of Mary, of whom that only absolute gentleman Jesus was born...and gentleman by his mother Mary princesse of coat armour."

"*The Booke of Armorie, The Gentleman's Academie,* or  *The Booke of S. Albans*...compiled by Juliana Bernes (1496) and now reduced into a better method by G(ervase) M(arkham)."        London, 1595.

*Maister of Defence* (183). The Elizabethan name for a Fencing Master: there was a Guild or *Mystery* of them (see Prologue, p. 23).

" My profession said *Vincentio* (Saviolo?) what is my profession.
Then said the gentleman, he is a Maister of the noble science of Defence."
" I speak not against Maisters of Defence indeed, they are to
be honoured, nor against the Science, it is noble, and in mine opiniō
to be preferred next to Diuinitie; for as Diuinitie preserueth the soule
from hell and the divell, so doth this noble Science defend the bodie
from wounds and slaughter."

" The Dagger serueth well at length to put by a thrust, and at the
halfe Sword to crosse the Sword-blade, to driue out the Agent, and put
him in danger of his life."          Silver's *Paradoxes of Defence.*

The equivoque in the text (183) consists in the dagger being always
used to parry or ward off the blow.

*Fencing School* (182).    "For of fence, almost in every town, there is
not only masters to teach it, with his provosts, ushers, scholars and
other names of art and school; but there hath not failed also, which
hath diligently and favouredly written it, and is set out in print, that
every man may read it.

*Philologe.*    But in learning of fence, I pray you what is that which
men most labour for?

*Toxophilus.*    That they may hit another, I trow, and never take
blow their self.

*Phil.*    But was there ever any of them so cunning yet, which, at
one time or other, hath not been touched.

*Tox.*    The best of them all is glad sometime to escape with a blow.

*Phil.*    Then in fence also, men are taught to go about that thing,
which the best of them all knoweth he shall never attain unto."

R. Ascham, *Toxophilus.*

*Fencing-Schoole.*    " Like him, who thought to come to bee a good
Fencer by looking on *Agrippa's* [or *Don Luis de Nervins'*] book-
postures only."

James Howell's *Instructions for Forreine Travell* 1642 (Arber).

" We travel into Italie to learne the art of fencing, and practise it at

the cost of our lives before we know it ; it were requisite according to
the order of true discipline, we should preferre the theorike before the
practike.   We betray our apprentissage."

Florio's Montaigne, ii. 37.

*Prize* (295).   "You have play'd your Prize."

*Titus Andronicus*, i. 1. 399.

"Like the Usher of a Fence-schoole, about to play his prize."

Greene's *Quip for an Upstart Courtier*.

*Archery* (185).  "Amongst all the English artillery, *Archerie* challengeth
the pre-heminence...first shewed to the English by the *Danes*, brought
in by the *Normans*, continued by their Successors to the great glory of
*England*, in atchieving honourable victories ; but now dispossessed by
gunnery, how justly let others judge.   Much may be said for either."

Camden, *Remaines concerning Britaine*.

"Milice redoubtable :  la fleur des archiers du monde."

Ph. de Comines on English Bowmen.

> "*In Praise of Archery.*
> Brave Archery, what rapture shall I raise
> In giving thee thy merit, and due praise
> So ancient, so divine, so nobly fam'd ;
> (Yet for the bodie's health there's nothing nam'd.)
> It is an Exercise (by proofe) we see
> Whose practise does with nature best agree.
> Obstructions from the liver it prevents,
> Stretching the Nerves and Art'rys gives extents
> To the spleenes oppilations, clears the brest
> And spungy lungs :  it is a foe profest
> To all consumptions :  More, what need I name ?
> The State approves it for a lawful game.
> What woon our honour, is now made our Sport,
> Witness Poicteirs, Cressy and Agincourt."

Th. Heywood, *Pleasant Dialogues and Drammas* (1637).

"The posture of the Bow and Arrow...hath affinitie with the Musquet and the postures of the Palizadoe, which is a good conduct to the Pike."

"Now if I shall be questioned touching the mixture of these seuerall weapons, the *Pike*, the *Musquet* and the Bow, or in what sort they may be imbattayled without disorder or hinderance of one weapon with another; I answer...I conceive it may be done both easily and profitably.

"In the days of Queen *Elizabeth* of thrice happy and blessed memory, when the use of the *Musquet* was newly brought from beyond the Seas unto this Kingdome, and the vertue thereof found and approved; yet was the weapon so scarce to be had, workemen so slow, and new alterations so unpleasant, that the State was compelled to compound their Bands of three seuerall Weapons, the *Pike*, *Musquet*, and the *Harquebush* or *Calliuer*, as I am able to shew by sundry lists."

Gervase Markham, *The Art of Archerie.*

NOTE. I would recommend to Toxophils the issuing a facsimile of this charming little 32mo with its old woodcut frontispiece of a Bowyer in action.

*Bow, Bill and Gun* (185). "In like maner when occasion is ministred to speak of shoting or archeri, we Englishmen may cal it the honour of our Country...Therfore it shal become al gentlemen to use this our English pastime of shoting for their greatest game and disport...Furthermore yf wee compare the warres of tymes passed wythe those whiche haue beene, synce the inuencion of the Gunne, we shall perceiue that the Valiency of men touching right manhead hath bene nothing like unto that auncient time."

*The Institucion of a Gentleman*, 1568.

*Bow Bill.* Invert the words and you have another pun 'Bilbow,' a fine Spanish blade manufactured at Bilbao.

"When down their bows they threw
And forth their *bilbows* drew."

Drayton's *Battle of Agincourt.*

"*Scholar.* What handling is proper to the instruments?
*Toxophilus.* Standing, nocking, drawing, holding and loosing, where-by cometh fair shooting, which belongeth neither to wind, nor weather."
                                                                    Ascham.

" For some shall maintain that a Turk can be hit at twelve score pricks in Finsbury Fields. *Ergo* the bow and shafts won Boulogne; others say that a pot-gun is a dangerous weapon against a mud-wall, and an enemy to the Painter's work."
        Taylor's *Penniless Parliament of Thread-Bare Poets*, 1608.

*Any man may bend him as he list* (190). " But again in stringing your bow, you must look for much bend or little bend, for they be clean contrary."                                         Ascham's *Toxophilus*.

*Nocke* (194), cf. the ballad *St George for England* by John Grubb, M.A., 1688, wherein King Arthur's sword " y-cleped Caliburn " was said to

> "Split a man at single slash
> From noddle down to *nock*."

*Nocke* stands for " breech ": which, the talk being of guns, might be taken by the less vulgar-minded as an Academic *a posteriori* prediction of the long delayed invention of the Breech-loader.

*Nocking the Arrow* is the time-honoured phrase for notching the arrow, see Hansard's *Book of Archery* 1896, where the process of " nocking" ("shifting your shaft-hand down to the nock ") is fully described.

" The nocke of the Shaft is diversly made, for some be great and full, some handsome and little, some wide, some narrow, some deepe, some shallow, some round, some long, some with one Nocke, some with a double Nocke whereof euery one hath his seuerall property."
        Ascham's *Toxophilus* copied by G.M. *The Art of Archerie*, 1634.

" First in putting the Nock betweene your two first fingers, then bringing the Shaft under the String and over the Bow, then to set the Shaft neither too high nor too low, but euen and straight ouer-thwart the Bow."                                         *Ibid.*

<u>*Bill*</u> (195).   " The Forrest Bill is a double weapon by reason of the head, and therefore hath eight wardes, foure with the staffe, foure with the heade."

" The Welch hooke or Forrest Bill, hath advantage against all maner of weapons whatsoever."

" The Halbard or blacke Bill, or such like weapons of weight, ap perteining unto guard or battell."                         Silver.

" When English men used *Hercules* weapons, the bow and the black bill, they fought victoriously with *Hercules* success : so I hope they shall carry way no victory more happily now, when they adjoin to those weapons of *Hercules*, *Iove's* thunder-bolt ; for so some now call our greatshot."                         Camden's *Remaines*, 1605.

" *The Bill* (A.-S. *byll*, Irish *biail*, *securis*, German *Beil* = Axe) was introduced into England *temp*. Henry VI. about the fifteenth century, when it was allied in form to the Halbard.   Skinner considers it a *securis rostrata* (beaked axe).   It was long a favourite in Scandinavia, and the illustration (Fig. 101) represents the weapon of Gunnar, the Icelandic Champion, which sang before battle, as also did the Sword of Sigard."                         Burton, *Book of the Sword*, p. 95.

<u>*Bill's a Tall-fellow ons hands*</u> (200).   " As he lived in a ruffling time, so he loved sword and buckler men, and such as our Fathers were wont to call men of their hands."

Sir Robert Naunton, *Fragmenta Regalia*.

(Lord Hunsdon) 1641 (Arber's Edition).

*Tall* ${of's \atop on's}$ } hands, *i.e.* of his inches : hand = 4 in.

See also Nares' *Glossary*, *Merry Wives of Windsor* I. 4. 27 and *Winter's Tale* v. 2. 181.

" To know the perfect length of your short staffe, or half Pike, Forrest bil, Partisan or Gleue (Glaive)...you shall stand upright, holding the staffe upright close by your body, with your left hand, reaching with your right hand your staffe as high as you can, and then allow to that length a space to set both your hands, when you come to fight;

wherein you may conueniently strike, thrust and ward, and that is the just length to be made according to your stature."

Silver's *Paradoxes of Defence.*

*Bill, Ile pay him* (197).

Ben Jonson has the same pun in *The Staple of News* upon the duns of Pennyboy Canter:

"Do I not muster a brave troop, all billmen?...Good bills, sufficient bills, these bills may pass.  (*Puts them in his pockets.*)"

"Argent, three *Bils* in Pale, Sable, name of Gibbes."

Gwillim's *Display of Heraldrie,* 1610.

"I abhor bills in a morning.

*Pen.*  Your honour says true:
Their knavery will be discern'd by daylight;
But thou may'st watch at night with bill in hand
And no man dares find fault with it."

Nat. Field, *A woman is a weathercock.*

*Will quickly be Wood* (201).

"Cardinal Wolsey, I say, waxed so wood therewith, that he studied to invent all ways of revengement against the Emperor."

William Roper: *The Mirrour of Vertue in Worldly Greatness, or the Life of Sir Thomas More Knight.*

"**Wood**, *or in a rage,* as the winde doth in the wood, *ex Belg:* **woed**, **woede**, *furor, rabies, insania:* **woeder** *quod vet.* Sax: et Sicambr, pro Tyranno."    John Minsheu, *The Guide into the Tongues.*  1617.

(Francis Bacon was one of the Subscribers to this work, the first which contained a printed list.)

*Gunne* (203).    "The earliest mention of hand-guns occurs in connection with Perugia as early as 1364 (Clephan).  The first portable fire-arm, or small hand-cannon, is of the same date as the breech-loading cannon, both being invented at the beginning of the 14th century."  Demmin.  (See note to *Flash*, p. 77.)

"Yet of all weapons, the best is, as Euripides doth say, wherewith with least danger of ourself, we may hurt our enemy most. And that is, (as I suppose) artillery. Artillery now-a-days, is taken for two things, guns and bows."                                                   Ascham.

"And therefore banish not onely from your Court all traiterous offensiue weapons, forbidden by the Lawes, as guns and such like...but also all traiterous defensiue armes, as secrets, plade sleeves and such like unseene armour[1]."                          James I., *Basilikon Doron.*

"Having names given them, some from Serpents or ravenous birds, as Culverines or Colubrines, Serpentines, Basilisques, Faulcons, Sacres; others in other respects as Canons, Demi Canons, Chambers, Slingis, Arquebuze, Caliver Handgun, Muskets, Petronils, Pistoll, Dagge &c. and Petarvas of the same brood lately invented."

Camden's *Remaines,* 1605.   (Artillerie.)

"True it is that Mosquets being in the hands of skilful Mosquettiers are of great effect for divers purposes; and that kind of weapon of that length with restes, and so ranforced, was first used in *Italie* above 60 years past (i.e. circa 1530) as I have divers times heard auncient Captaines of the *Italian* and *Spanish* Nation say."

He continues: "the Duke of Alva when Governor of the Low Countries increased the number of Foot Musketeers to counteract the effect of the *Ratters*" (? Reiters).

Sir John Smythe, *Discourses* etc. (see note on p. 28 for full title).

*Bouncing* (202).   Ben Jonson of a woman:

"A very *bona Roba* and a Bouncer."

*The New Inn*, Act III. Sc. 2.

"Is your Italian the finest gentleman?—In the world, Signor. Your Spaniard is a mere Bumbard to him: he will bounce indeed but he will burst."                     Heywood's *Four Prentices.*

Here bounce signifies the recoil of a piece of ordnance (Bumbard), much as in the text, and our modern "Bounder" may be derived from the rebound or 'bounce' of the Elizabethan gun.

---

[1] See also Viscount Dillon, *Archæologia*, Vol. LI., on Guns in the Tower.

*Dagger in Cheape* (285).

In a Descriptive Catalogue of the London Traders, Tavern, and Coffee-House Tokens current in the 17th Century, by J. H. Burn, 1853, we find the following :—

"*At the Dagar and (Pie)*.   A Dagger ; magpie on point.   *Reverse* : Pye in Foster Lane (Cheapside).   In the field M. H. D."

" Richard Smith, in his Obituary, Sloane MS. 886, records :

Decr. 22, 1657, Moses Dannet at ye Dagger in Foster Lane buried."

I have come to the conclusion that the " Dagger in Cheape " (far less frequently mentioned in Elizabethan literature than its namesake in Holborn) must have been situate in Foster Lane, Cheapside : see Notes on " Dagger," " Dagger Ale," &c.

" O gentle fellow-soldiers, then leave your controversies, if you love a woman, for I will prove it that a mince-pie is better than a musket ; and he that dare gainsay me, let him meet me at the Dagger in Cheape, with a case of pewter spoons, and I will answer it."

Taylor's *Pennilesse Parliament of thread-bare Poets*, 1608.

C. Hindley's edition, 1872.

See also Hobson's *Jests*, 1607.

" 2nd *Pren*.   I must needs step to the Dagger in Cheap to send a letter into the Country unto my Father.   Stand by ; you are the youngest 'prentice, look you to the shop."

Thos. Heywood's *If you know not me etc.*

"...Ten pounds in a morning? here's the fruit
Of Dagger-pies and ale-house guzzlings."

" In Vol. 2 of *Extracts from the Stationers' Registers*, p. 171, is mentioned the publication of *A fancie on the fall of the Dagger in Cheap*, which may mean either that the house, or the sign which it bore, fell down ; probably the latter, although the Editor, in his note on the entry, supposed that the word 'fall' applied to the house."

J. P. Collier's Note.

There was another " Dagger " in Holborn frequented by gamblers and sharpers (Nares) celebrated for its Dagger-pies and Dagger-ale (see B. Jonson's *Alchemist* I. I, Fulwell's *Art of Flatterie, Witt's Recreation*, and Gascoigne's *Del. Diet for Droonkards* and Dekker's *Satiromastix*).

In Greene's *Arcadia or Menaphon* he speaks of " Dagger Drunkenness " on a " pot of blew burning ale, with a fiery flaming toste." Egerton Brydges' *Censura Litteraria*, vol. VII. p. 165.

*Gunpowder Plot.* 1605 (228). In a tract dated 1606 (reprinted in C. Hindley's *Old Book Collectors' Miscellany*) on the Arraign and Execution of the late Traitors (four at St Paul's Churchyard on Thursday 30th Jan., and four in the old Palace in Westminster over against the Parliament house on Friday following), "Fawkes, the minor, justly called, the Devil of the Vault " is spoken of as " alias Johnson."

*Powder* (209). "When the Letter was shewed to me by my Secretary, wheren a generall obscure aduertisement was given of some dangerous blow at this time, I did upon the instant interpret and apprehend some darke phrases therein, (contrary to the ordinary Grammer construction of them, and in an other sort then I am sure any Divine, or Lawyer in any Universitie would have taken them) to be meant by this horrible forme of blowing us all up by powder."

K. James I., A speech in Parliament, 1605.

"*Pen.* If you cross him, he'll blow you up with gunpowder.

*Abra.* In good faith, he looks as if he had had a hand in the treason. I'll take my leave."

Nat. Field, *A woman is a weathercock.*

*Parliament House* (230). " Surely if I were one of the Parliament-house, I would not fail to put up a bill for the amendment of this thing."

Ascham's *Toxophilus.*

*Flash* (219). "Sir Petronel *Flash*" was a name given to a Braggadocio or boasting fellow.

"*Pietranelli* souldiers serving on horseback armed with *petronels*, snaphances or fire-lock pieces and cuirasses." (Florio.)

"Petronel (from *Poitrinal*) = Hand-Cannon for a Knight."
        H. B. Wheatley's Note to *Every man in his Humour*.

<u>*Shyre*</u> (223). See Thos. Hearne's *Curious Discourses* (Of what antiquity Shires were in England) by Several Hands.

"The other House is composed of Knights for the Shire and Gentry, and Burgesses for the Townes."
        James I. A speach in Parliament, 1605.

On the 27th Nov. 1616 that prince of hack-writers (and riders), Gervase Markham, was censured in the Star Chamber and fined in the sum of £500 for sending a challenge to Lord Davey. The quarrel between them arose from his Lordship's dog "Bowser" having been "in danger to be trodden on" by Markham at a hunting party at Sir Gervase Clifton's. Opinions were delivered by the King's Attorney, the Chancellor of the Exchequer, the Lord Chief Justice, Secretary Winwood, the Vice-Chamberlain, the Bishops of Ely and London, the Master of the Wards, Lord Arundell, the Lord Treasurer, the Archbishop of Canterbury and the Lord Chancellor. *Censura Litteraria*, vol. III. p. 64. See curious anecdote of encounter between G. M. and Sir John Holles in 1597 in *Theatr. Poet. Ang.* (279—80), copied from Collins's *Noble Families* 84, 5.

See also 2 *State Trials* 743 and Prologue (p. 29) for the prosecution of Lord Sanquhar for the murder of the Fencing Master (Turner) "who had accidentally put out one of the northern Pier's Eyes in playing at Rapier and Dagger," in which Bacon as Solicitor General conducted the prosecution.
        Lord Campbell, *Lives of the Chancellors*, vol. II. p. 329.

<u>*Backe-Friend to us both*</u> (257). So Hobbes of Chillingworth : "A lusty fellow that would drive his enemies before him ; but would often give his own party a shrewd backblow."

*Long Sword* (287). "Logic is the armoury of reason, furnished with all offensive and defensive weapons. There are syllogisms, long swords; enthymemes, short daggers; dilemmas, two-edged swords, that cut on both sides; sorites, chain-shot; and for the defensive, distinctions, which are shields; retortions, which are targets with a pike in the midst of them, both to defend and oppose."

Thos. Fuller, D.D., *The Holy State* (The General Artist).

Also, "Fencing is war without anger; and manly sports are the grammar of military performances." Ibid. "Of Recreations."

*Field and Fields* (37), (242). These words so frequent of occurrence have a general and special sense: *the field*, generally, standing for the field of combat or *terrain*; and *Fields* being the unbuilt-over spaces in and around London, especially on the North side. If we look at Ralph Agas's Map of London (Civitas Londinum) date about 1560, we see that the Fields bounded the whole of the North side of London, behind Holborn: there, in order, we find *Schmyt Fyeld* (Smithfield), *More Fyeld* (Moorfields), *Fynesbury Fyeld* (Finsbury Field) and *The Spurl-Fyeld* (Spitalfields), of which we learn the following particulars from Stow and other sources:—

*Smithfield* or Smoothfield, the *planus Campus re et nomine* of Fitz-stephen.

"And this Sommer 1615 [the year of our play] the Citty of London reduced the rude vast place of Smithfield into a fair and comely order, which formerly was neuer held possible to be done, and paued it all ouer...they also made strong rayles...and sequestred the middle part of the said Smithfield into a very faire and ciuill walk...And this field was for many yeares called 'Ruffian's Hall,' by reason it was the usual place of frayes, and common fighting during the time that sword and bucklers were in use. But the ensuing deadly fight of Rapier and Dagger suddenly suppressed the fighting with Sword and Buckler."

Howes' ed. of Stowe, 1631, p. 1023. See Cunningham's *Handbook of London*, Wheatley's edition.

"I'll buy this i' the field, so I will; I have a mind to it, because 'tis a field rapier."

> B. Jonson, *Every Man in his Humour*, Act II. Sc. 2.

"Neither to look back to the Sword and Buckler age of Smithfield, but content himself with the present."

> B. J., Induction to *Bartholomew Fair*.

Stowe notes the encroachments and enclosure of this S., "whereby remaineth but a small portion for the old uses; to wit for markets of horses and cattle, neither for military exercises, as joustings, turnings and great triumphs, which have been there performed before the princes and nobility, both of this realm and foreign countries" [see Froissart].

*St Giles in the Fields.* "Ye may read in mine annals how that in the year 1222 the citizens kept games of defence, and wrestlings, near unto the hospital of St Giles in the field, where they challenged and had the mastery of the men in the suburbs and other commoners...The youths of this city also have used on holy days after Evening prayer, at their masters' doors, to exercise their wasters and bucklers." Stow's *Survey* p. 36. Strutt, *Sports and pastimes* Bk III. Chap. VI. Sec. 22, gives an engraving of this.

*Tothill Fields* (or Fields, on the south side of the Thames). Minsheu's Dictionary 1617.

> "*Spendall.*   And I will meet thee in the field as fairly
>            As the best gentleman that wears a Sword.
>   *Stainer.*   I accept it : the meeting Place?
>   *Spendall.*   Beyond the Maze in Tattle.
>     *St.*   What weapon? *Sp.* Single Rapier."

> *Greene's Tu quoque*, published by Thos. Heywood, 1614.

*Fields.* "It is also a kind of dastardliness which hath brought this fashion into our single combates, to accompany us in the fields with seconds, thirdes and fourths. They were anciently single combates, but now they are skirmishes and battels."

> Florio's Montaigne Bk II. chap. XXVII.
> (*Cowardize the Mother of Cruelty.*)

*Moorfields.* "This field of old time was called the More, as appeareth by the Charter of Wm. the Conqueror to the College of St Martin, declaring a running water to pass into the City from the same More. Also Fitzstephen writeth of this More saying thus: 'When the great Fen or moor, which watereth the walls on the North side is frozen &c.' This fen or moor field, stretching from the wall of the city betwixt Bishopsgate and the postern called Cripples gate to Fensbery and to Holy Well, continued a waste and unprofitable ground a long time [but in the year 1415 the Mayor built the postern called Moregate and caused the ditches to be cleansed and so drained and dried the fen]. In the year 1498 all the gardens, which had continued time out of mind without Moregate...were destroyed; and of them was made a plain field for archers to shoot in " [they may be descried in Agas]. Stow's *Survey.*

It was one of the chief resorts for duelling:—

"Walk into Moorfields.
I dare look on your Toledo. Do not shew
A foolish vapour in the Streets."
Massinger's *City Madam.*

Pepys stood and saw the wrestling there in 1661 and tells of the fray between the butchers and the weavers in 1664. It was the mustering ground of troops. Shadwell mentions cudgel-players and Tom Brown the second-hand booksellers under the trees, while Keats was born at livery-stables on the Pavement in Moorfields.

*Finsbury* or Fensbury without the posterns of Cripplegate and Moorgate lent its name to the Square and Circus which subsequently overspread Moorfields. Grub Street was hard by, "of late years inhabited for the most part by bowyers, fletchers, bowstring makers and such like occupations, now little occupied; archery giving place to a number of bowling alleys, and dicing houses, which in all places are increased and too much frequented." Stow.

The first Playhouse in London, "The Theatre," was erected in

Finsbury Fields in 1576, see *Early London Theatres* (*In the Fields*) by T. Fairman Ordish, F.S.A., who quotes from *Remembrancia* some interesting notices of fencing and sword play.

*Velvet* (275). See note to *Gilt* on p. 58, also on p. 20.

*Justice of the Peace* (101). James has himself told us how highly he valued the services of a Justice of the Peace, and we might almost suppose Dagger to have had an inkling of this from the dramatic effect of his announcement:

So let the Judges bee neuer so carefull and industrious, if the Justices of Peace vnder them, put not to their helping hands, in vaine is all your labour: For they are the Kings eyes and eares in the countrey...For I hold a good Justice of Peace in his Countrey, to doe mee as good seruice, as he that waites vpon mee in my Priuie Chamber, and as ready will I be to reward him; For I accompt him as capable of any Honour, Office, or preferment about my person, or for any place of Councell or State, as well as any Courteour that is neere about mee, or any that have deserued well of me in forreine employments: Yea, I esteeme the seruice done me by a good Justice of Peace, three hundred miles, yea sixe hundred miles out of my sight, as well as the seruice done me in my presence: For as God hath giuen me large limits, so must I be carefull that my prouidence may reach to the farthest parts of them. And as Law cannot be honoured, except Honour be given to Judges: so without due respect to Justices of Peace, what regard will be had of the seruice?

Therefore let none to be ashamed of this office, or be discouraged in being a Justice of Peace, if he serue worthily in it.

James I., Works, *A Speach in the Starre-chamber*, anno 1616.

*Philalethes.* Right. And from thence I infer, That Duelling is a very dishonourable Practice. For when you have given the best Proof of your Sufficiency, and killed your Man, you are seized into the Hands of Justice; treated like Assassins: and condemned to Die with Circumstances of Ignominy. You are not indicted for acquitting yourselves like Gentlemen; but for disturbing the Publick Peace, and murthering the King's Subjects. Now the Law never loads a Man with Reproaches, nor punishes him thus coarsely, for doing a handsome action.

*Essays upon Several Moral Subjects*, by Jeremy Collier, M.A., 1722.

So that it alwaies had a vigilant eye by anticipation to prevent many others that would breake the peace by any of the meanes aforesaid, and therefore hath from age to age appointed meet magistrates and watchmen, to whose charge especially (as Selected Sentinells) they bid commit the preservation of the peace, who in times past before the raigne of King Edward the Third, were called Conservators of the peace, and thence they have been termed Justices of peace, because they be Justices of Record, or otherwise they be named Commissioners of the Peace, because they have and derive their authority by the King's Commission who himselfe being the chiefe and generall Conservator and Preserver of the peace throughout all his dominions, doth by his severall Commissions commit some particles of his authoritie, touching the continuance of the peace, and maintenance of certain of his Lawes, to some chiefe and select men in all the parts of the Realme, whom hee taketh to bee the most miete men for the same in respect of their integrity, wisedome, learning, courage, and livelyhood.

Ferdinand Pulton of Lincoln's Inn, Esqre, *De Pace Regis.* 1623. Black Letter.

## EXTRACTS FROM

### A PUBLICATION OF HIS MA[TIES] EDICT AGAINST PRIVATE COMBATS, &c.

(See *Prologue*, pp. 30—33.)

Touching the first branch of actuall offences by Blowes with the hand, Stripes with a rod, Bruises with a cudgell, stabbes with a Dagger, or hurts with a Rapier, Our purpose is out of the sense of Honour, to extend Our punishment as far aboue those ordinary degrees, which are now in vse, as the facts themselues exceede all humanitie. For though the differences betweene greater and lesser occasions and motiues cannot bee denied, and the *Ciuilians* distinguish by their Lawes betweene Blowes that smart, or smart not; yet since that scorne holdes a Gentleman well borne, and sutably behaued, worthy the chastisement of a dog, this onely respect ought to bee preferred to the smart that is felt by the sences......

This *Striker* shall condemne vnder his owne hand, before hee bee suffered to depart out of restraint, that saucie *Paradox* which giues liberty to Gentlemen with their owne Swordes to reuenge wrongs done to themselues. Hee shall further promise solemnly before the Lords, neuer to offend vpon the like occasion, in the like contempt. Hee shall be bound to the good Behauiour during the space of the next sixe Moneths that ensue, and during the same terme likewise abstaine from Our Court, and from all places where the *Queene* our dearest Spouse, and the *Prince* Our dearest Sonne shal happen to reside. For it is true that *Palaces* of this qualitie, should rather serue for so many *Sanctuaries* to distressed Subiects that endure wrong, then receptacles or retraits for persons of vnstayed iudgement, that offer it. Last of all, Wee leaue the person that was hurt or stricken, to the benefit of his action of *Battery* at the Common Lawe, with a meaning, that Our Censures be reputed rather *cumulatiue*, then *priuatiue*, of any lawfull help that Iustice yeeldes, vnlesse the Lordes can deuise by their discretion at the cleansing of the wound, to purge all motiues that may cause it by succeeding accidents, (that rancle and renew) to breake out againe.......

For triall of the maine point, after Gentlemen haue agreed to trie the Quarrell by their Swords in the Field, it is considerable whether both of them be slaine or neither. For in euery one of these, the diuersitie of Degrees drawes in likewise a great difference betweene the courses that are to bee obserued by the Lords, and their Deputies. Touching the partie slaine after *Challenge* in cold blood by single Fight, in despite of Our decree, or in case the match consist of many, touching all those that are slaine, Our part is onely to leaue them to the Iustice or Mercie of their *Eternall Iudge*.......

In excuse of Seconds, it is said by some, that they were onely brought in as vsefull instruments to paire weapons, to search bodies, to depart the *Combatants* vpon equall tearmes, to suppresse aduantage vpon either side, and to see faire play : yet since the Fight it selfe is absolutely bad in it selfe, it is not possible for any acte assisting, or abetting, whatsoeuer cloud be cast vpon a tender eye, to bee iust, or in a matter of this weight to warrant accessaries, when We taxe the principall. These Seconds in very deed, to make the best of them, are onely stout Assistants to bad ends : their fairest actions are but formall preparations : their excuses are but shadowes : though they see the sinner, yet they runne with him. If wee marke well, their labours and endeuours are of little vse : For whatsoeuer be expected of their Humanitie, their Charitie and Care ; yet whosoeuer vndertakes to moderate men in fight will not forbeare, either vpon the sight of blood, or the sence of smart, to rush desperately vpon extremities. These Seconds might perhaps serue better to some ende, in case the prosecution of priuate Quarrels by the Sword, were first admitted and approoued by any *Prince* or *State* : But since they shrinke that should bee the Supports and Stayes, it is not strange, that *Sublato Principali, omnia cadunt accessoria* : Betweene an Actor therefore and an Abettor, the difference cannot bee great, howsoeuer malice may be masked vnder false couers.......

The better to bring Quarrels to discouerie, when they begin first to worke, it is obserued, that not onely in the common Ordinaries, to which Gentlemen doe vsually resort, but sometimes also in the Tennis Courts, in bowling Allies, Dicing houses, and all houses of game, questions sometimes vpon a cast, sometimes vpon distemper in losse, vpon refusall to lend vpon importunitie to be paid, vpon termes of comparison, and words of exception, vpon as many contingents, as places of that nature breed vexations and contradictions.......

# *Glossarial Epilogue* 85

For remedie whereof, Wee doe straitly charge and command; First Our owne Groome-porter, and then all other keepers of gaming-houses, of Tennis Courts, and bowling Allies, vpon paine of Our high displeasure, beside three moneths commitment and suspension of their power, to keepe houses of resort to that end, for the space of three whole yeeres at the least, that instantly vpon the giuing of any reproachful word, or passing any blow betweene Gentlemen, that are likelie to seeke a sharpe reuenge by the sword, in some place more priuate, their first care bee to take the weapons of the persons kindled with rage, if it may be; the next to keepe them in sunder till some Officer of the Peace be brought into the place to command in Our name, till the Quarrell comming to the hearing of the Lords in Commission, may receiue a sharper censure, or a better satisfaction, as they in their graue Iudgements shall finde, both the persons to deserue, and the cause to be considerable.

# INDEX.

CAMBRIDGE: PRINTED BY J. AND C. F. CLAY, AT THE UNIVERSITY PRESS.

Lightning Source UK Ltd.
Milton Keynes UK
UKHW040611190919
350067UK00001B/20/P

9 781108 003117